' the conversations '
66 reasons to start talking

' the conversations '
66 reasons to start talking

OLIVIA FANE

◨ SQUARE PEG

Published by Square Peg 2013

2 4 6 8 10 9 7 5 3 1

Copyright © Olivia Fane 2013

First published in Great Britain in 2013 by Square Peg
Random House, 20 Vauxhall Bridge Road, London SW1V 2SA

www.vintage-books.co.uk

Addresses for companies within The Random House Group Limited can
be found at: www.randomhouse.co.uk/offices.htm

The Random House Group Limited Reg. No. 954009

A CIP catalogue record for this book is available from the British Library

ISBN 9780224095693

The Random House Group Limited supports The Forest Stewardship
Council® (FSC®), the leading international forest-certification
organisation. Our books carrying the FSC label are printed on FSC®-
certified paper. FSC is the only forest-certification scheme supported by
the leading environmental organisations, including Greenpeace. Our paper
procurement policy can be found at www.randomhouse.co.uk/environment

In memory of my mother

contents

❛ an introduction ❜

I am writing this book for my former self, the young woman who wondered soon after her first marriage at the age of twenty-two to the cleverest, wittiest man she had ever met: why aren't we having the really good conversations we used to have when we first went out together?

I looked back at the days he courted me. Once, I remember, he drove me up to the west coast of Scotland. There seemed to be no landscape that he didn't know intimately: the battles fought there, the massacres, the exact route of the flight of Bonnie Prince Charlie. I listened, rapt, and fell in love with him. A few years later long car journeys happened in silence, punctuated only by a little family gossip and domestic arrangements. This was not what I'd had in mind.

Where does conversation go to when you've been with the same partner for a long time? Does it really have to just peter out, as though human beings were finite containers, the contents of which simply get used up over time? No wonder there are some who suggest that marriages should end after five years as a matter of course – a sort of 'been there, done that' description of what it's like to share your life intimately with someone else. And this was exactly how it felt to me: that I'd been used up.

My first marriage lasted seven years; when I married a second time three years later I was determined to be more alert. I was curious to know what marriage was made of, so to speak. I wanted to be aware of its very grain, close up. And I wanted to keep this one for life.

And yet here was the strangest thing: what I found myself missing in those early months were those periods of *not* talking, of knowing my partner so well and feeling so comfortable with him I might have been living on my own. Suddenly here I was with this *other person* to whom I consciously had to relate. How very tiring that was – for both of us, I believe. Suddenly there was *someone else* in the bathroom, and when I used the bathroom, a question popped into my head that I hadn't known for years: to lock or not to lock?

So at first, when we stopped having conversations, as inevitably we did, it seemed like progress. When I first forgot to lock the bathroom door, I never locked it again. When we spent long car journeys listening to Radio 3 I didn't mind, because by then I knew that intimacy was more important than chatter. My husband inherited three young sons from my first marriage, and we had two more. We were both too physically exhausted to consider *us* in any meaningful way. And then last year, after twenty-eight years of motherhood, my youngest child went off to boarding school. Finally we could hear ourselves speak, and we had, quite tentatively, our first 'real' conversation in years. We made a time and a space for it: 8 p.m. on our first childless Monday. We were to read – together – two pages of Kierkegaard comparing romantic with conjugal love. We lay on the sofa together – my husband's feet beside my head – and began to talk. Suddenly the man I was talking to was not just my husband of eighteen years but the *other person* who had entered my life so many years previously as a stranger. And now, it seemed, I had the best of all worlds – both intimacy and otherness in one, a perfect playmate.

We had known each other as undergraduates: all those years ago we doubtless had conversations about politics and religion, all the normal stuff. But after thirty years of *living* had our attitudes changed? What had we learnt not from books but just from being-in-the-world? The thrill was that we had both learnt a good deal without realising it, and even though we were out of practice, the art of conversation was a skill we soon picked up again with a relish I would not have thought possible.

The word for 'love' in Greek is *eros*, and etymologically is closely connected to the Greek word to 'ask questions' – *erotao*. I love this fact. To ask someone questions is to be hungry to get to know them, there is an energy implicit in the Greek, and to know them is to love them. In romantic love, you love a fiction, an ideal. In conjugal love, you love over time. In Kierkegaard's words, and those we read that first evening together, 'Conjugal love has its foe in time, its triumph in time, its eternity in time.' In the Ages of Man everything is downhill: once there was a mythical Golden Age, the Age of Heroes, and then the Silver, and the Bronze. In marriage, we proceed from paper and cotton to silver, gold, rubies and diamonds. A shared history, a shared knowledge, an understanding and acceptance of what is still, and excitingly so, *other*: these are the prizes of the long haul.

I am shamelessly honest and frank, and come from a long line of shamelessly honest and frank forebears, especially my mother, to whom this book is dedicated. In her lifetime, her fearlessness in confronting the taboo made her many enemies, and perhaps my directness will seem alarming to some. But even if I become your common enemy, my mission shall be accomplished.

Yet conversations don't just bring partners together. We all love to talk about things that matter. This book is for everyone who likes to ask and be asked questions: friends, siblings, new dates, inquisitive teenagers. It's even for people to enjoy, as I do, asking themselves questions. For as long as I can remember, I've had my bath in the dark, a warm, soothing place for a soak and a good think.

It's been a pleasure to write these conversations and of course I hope they are a 'good read'. But with all my heart I want them to be more than that. I want people to really give them a go. Make them an evening's entertainment, a game with no winners or losers, a game with a sofa and a glass of wine. The joy of really getting to know another human being is greater, even, than sex.

' on happiness '

I read a good definition of happiness the other day: 'subjective well-being'. If you can count yourself as happy, then you are.

The night before I gave birth to my first son I had a dream, in which I was given a choice. Either I would wish him happiness: nothing too bad would ever happen to him, he would have a secure job, marry and have children. None of his children would die before him, and his wife and he would spend many happy days playing sport, watching TV and seeing friends. Or I could wish for him a life of truth, in which our ultimately wretched human condition would be revealed to him. On the back of such an understanding, he would be a great writer and composer.

In the dream I wished my son every happiness, with a heavy heart.

Periodically, I go back to that dream. In fact, it has often seemed to me that the 'happy' life doesn't seem much of a life at all, barely worth a human breath. A huge 'So What?' hangs over it. When I meet happy people I immediately feel claustrophobic. They are full to the brim of 'subjective well-being' and nothing seems to quite touch them. There even seems to be an air of self-congratulation about their untouchability.

This might all seem rather gloomy; a life would be unbearable if we were made aware of others' sufferings every waking hour and could never know the simple delight of a beautiful morning and a crisp blue sky. Last Christmas a vicar suggested we should not wish each other 'Happy Christmas' until the world's wrongs had been righted, and we could *all* aspire to have a happy Christmas. Oh dear! To ban happiness on account of its inequality of distribution seems a fairly miserable way to carry on.

Yet happiness is interesting: to be worth having (in my view) it requires substance. Happiness is more than simply having a continuous outlet for hedonism. When I feel happy, I know that three conditions will have been met: I have to have a clear conscience, to be involved in a project or activity in which I feel I am making progress, and to be connected to those I love in an open and honest way. As I write this, numbers one and two need attention. I am good at the third.

What is curious about happiness is that it actually increases when you have known unhappiness. Soldiering on for ten years on your own, and then embarking on a true and intimate friendship, is more conducive to a deeper happiness than if you've had loads of friends all your life. Likewise if you're cured of some illness, saved from near death, or if you've just sighted land after months at sea: experiences such as these give a sense of gratitude that might last the rest of your life. I spent a fortnight in Albania a few years ago; I heard such stories of how people had suffered under the communist dictator Hoxha that when I came home I couldn't believe how fortunate I was. Everything seemed so beautiful and clean, people so friendly and trustworthy. I was on a high for months. It crossed my mind that all holidays should be spent in grisly tower blocks in over-populated cities: we would have fifty weeks of gratitude for our lot.

I've always been suspicious of easy solutions and self-help books which teach you how to be happy: forgive yourself! Move on! Stop feeling guilty! Think positively! No – I don't think so. I am much more of the school of Alcoholics Anonymous, who remind you to feel guilty and then make you go round apologising to everyone you've hurt. And I was impressed by the headmaster of Wellington College who suggested that the key to happiness was resilience: holding firm when the going gets tough, as of course it's bound to from time to time. True happiness is only possible when the foundations are properly in place – and that doesn't just mean health, friends and enough money: a degree of ballast is needed – moral fibre, as it used to be called.

One final thought: when you're a child, happiness is so uncomplicated. Winning a challenging netball match is enough for positive joy. But as you get older layers and layers of all sorts of feelings attach themselves to the most innocent of activities. Naked enthusiasm gives way to poignancy, to loss. No wonder people turn to drink for a quick fix. My recipe: love, confide, trust. It's a risky business, the pain of rejection unbearable. But intimacy with others makes life worth living and, dare I say it – it can actually make you happy.

food for thought

Q *Were you happy as a child?*

Q *Do you think happiness has more to do with circumstances or character?*

Q *When you come across other people who seem light and joyous – a glimpse of a couple kissing on a beach, teenagers going through a dance routine in the park – do you find their happiness contagious or does it make you aware of your own lack of it?*

Q *If someone asked you whether you considered your partner a 'happy' person, what would you say to them?*

Q *You have 48 hours to do exactly as you choose. Devise your perfect break.*

Q *Is a good conscience necessary to be truly happy?*

Q *Is it a good idea for schoolchildren to be taught how to be happy, or is 'being happy' a state beyond your control?*

❛ on the soul ❜
(according to plato)

When I was young I was ill for a week and was kept in isolation in the sanatorium at my boarding school. It was one of the most productive weeks of my entire education. This small building was set deep in the countryside, a mile away from the main school. In my bedroom was an old-fashioned stove, and the walls were lined with dark, polished wood. I spent my time writing poetry on crispy loo paper with the stub of an old pencil, and reading the only two books I could lay my hands on: a Greek textbook, and Plato's *Republic*.

I was sixteen and hungry to know what being-in-the-world was about, and Plato was the most exciting writer I had ever come across. I didn't read him critically, as an academic might, querying this and that, but as a plough-man might his Bible, on reading it for the first time. Every single word of it rang true, and it didn't occur to me to question anything Plato taught me. As far as I was concerned, I now knew what a soul was, I now understood what it was to be an 'I'.

Nowadays, of course, most of us (sadly) don't believe in

souls. In our view we have minds which can reason and we have bodies; ultimately everything can be reduced to bodies, as neurologists are forever telling us. We value, as a society, intelligence: logic, mathematics, science, computers, organisations; and we value, as a society, bodies: every aspect of physical beauty – fitness, sport, sex, eating and drinking. All else is suspect: at best, a waste of time (e.g. an education in the humanities) and at worst, plain stupid (e.g. a belief in 'intuition' or 'inappropriate' emotion, such as the mass 'hysteria' over Princess Diana's death. Yes, even mourning nowadays is considered in some way 'pathological').

But my beloved Plato, how wise he was! Rather than reducing everything to ultimately being about the body, he expanded everything to ultimately being about the soul. The 'I' who lusts, the 'I' who hungers, is the same 'I' who can write a computer program. But the third part of Plato's tripartite soul – alongside reason and appetite – is for me the most important part of us, and one that we in the modern world have all but forgotten: the part he calls *thumos*, a wonderfully untranslatable word, but so recognisable in us that the study of it should be part of the primary school curriculum.

The *thumos* is the nuclear core of the human being, without which we are computers that eat and have sex. It's the part of us which reacts before we've had the time to work out *why* we are reacting in a particular way. When I was a schoolgirl, we translated *thumos* as 'moral outrage', the part of you which knows immediately that something is awry even though you can't put your finger on it. Another translation is 'anger' – but a deep, justifiable anger, from one's very gut; or 'passion' – a quick and irrational understanding of something important. Plato simply describes it as that part in us which is neither rational nor appetitive: it is about 'everything else' – its function is to complete the picture of us as human beings. In his dialogue *Phaedrus* Plato gives *thumos* a more important role yet: it has glimpsed heaven and yearns to return there, recognising the beauty in this world as a reflection of something even more perfect. *Thumos* is, therefore, the feeling in us which gives rise to romantic love, or religious yearning, or a desire for justice. It is the feeling which yearns for more; that refuses to be satisfied with the mundane.

But Plato doesn't give *thumos* a free rein. He compares the harmonious soul to a charioteer (reason) achieving mastery over two horses (appetite and *thumos*): both the appetite and the *thumos* need to be kept in train; but reason can't act alone, it simply has no direction, no mojo, if you like. The rational and irrational parts in us have to work as a team. Now, where is the modern psychologist who's ever said anything wiser than that?

food for thought

Q *Think of a time when you were aware of the part of your soul which Plato calls* thumos. *Were your feelings positive or negative?*

Q *Do you agree that modern society tries to downplay this part of ourselves?*

Q *Recently a friend of mine had to read an academic paper called 'Lesbianism and the Fugue'. Do you see*

any justification in reading sexual drives into human activities which are not explicitly sexual?

Q *Would you say the three parts of your soul were well balanced? If not, which is the dominant part?*

Q *Would you say that your partner's soul was well balanced? If not, which would you say was the dominant part in him / her?*

Q *Aristotle thought it was possible to change one's character by acquiring better habits. Do you think he's right?*

Q *What practical action might you take to achieve a better balance in your tripartite soul?*

‘ on suicide ’

While other children were taken to pantomimes, my mother took me to see Tom Conti in *Whose Life is it Anyway?*, a play about a sculptor paralysed from the neck down who wants to end his life. Not just once, but twice. She said to me, 'Never, ever let that happen to me.' Needless to say, I failed her. She took two years to die, slowly, miserably, but I've never regretted not helping her to do so. What I do regret, however, is the failure of her suicide attempt, made at a time when she was still in full possession of her faculties. She was in a coma for 48 hours: she had not taken *quite* enough pills to finish herself off. When she came to, we commiserated with her; nonetheless, we dutifully made sure that pills were kept out of reach. Therein lies my self-recrimination. We should have made suicide easier for her, not more difficult.

Last year five thousand people killed themselves in the UK. A good friend of mine, a doctor, rages at them. 'How many lives are they ruining?' she asks me. Yet my own sympathy has always been with the victim. Because, in my eyes, someone who endures such a level of despair that their only option is to die is always a victim, and a victim of ourselves, the strong ones, the survivors.

Society puts such pressure on us all to succeed: to look good, to earn money, to run a thriving business, to be happy in our family life. When all of this conspires against you, when the money stops coming in, when your partner finds someone else, when your children have been poisoned against you, it's hard to imagine that you can ever pull yourself back. What an empty game this life must feel. With all my heart, I'm with them. Yet when an otherwise healthy person takes their own life, it can only ever be tragic both as a thing itself and for those left behind.

Yet sometimes suicide shouldn't be seen as a mad, desperate act but as something rational and brave. We should all understand it, come to terms with it, and even welcome it. The modern orthodoxy goes, 'It is always irrational to want to take your own life. You must be depressed and need pills.' What a load of hokum. What if you've been recently diagnosed with Alzheimer's, and within a few months you won't recognise your own children? What if you're a 23-year-old tetraplegic, whose passion in life before your accident was rugby? And as for those who argue that these people are somehow *ill* in their desire for death, and they should simply be given a course of anti-depressants until they get the 'right' answer, have they no sympathy, have they no imagination? The young rugby player Daniel James attempted suicide three times before he persuaded his parents to take him to the Dignitas clinic in Switzerland. On one of those occasions he attempted to stab himself. The psychiatrists who examined him found him to be in his right mind. Should we really be chivvying him along with, 'Look at so-and-so, he had an accident too and he went off to do a law degree!' Can't we recognise that Daniel James might not have wanted to do law? Nor might he have wanted to spend the next sixty years of his life in front of the TV, nor be the object of everyone's pity.

When, I wonder, will we as a society realise that suicide might be the *right* decision? When will we finally remove its stigma? When will we be able to say goodbye to our relatives without fearing that we're going to be harassed by the police? I for one have a cache of pills stored up in case the doctors diagnose something rotten. If I'm told, 'You'd have died long ago if it wasn't for modern medicine. We've given you ten healthy years, but my God you're going to suffer in the next ten!' Well, I'm sorry. Call it lack of gratitude, but I'm off.

Having watched my mother die, there is nothing I will not do to avoid going the same way. I've collected the right number of pills this time, more than enough. I've already said no to cervical smears and mammograms – why should I want my health to be screened if I'm going to end up in the same dreadful place as my mother?

The eighteenth-century philosopher David Hume wrote, 'If it be no crime, both prudence and courage should engage us to rid ourselves at once of existence when it becomes a burden. It is the only way that we can then be useful to society, by setting an example, which, if imitated, would preserve to everyone his chance of happiness in life, and would effectually free him from all danger or misery.'

It's an odd paradox that the willingness to kill yourself sets you free.

food for thought

Q *How bad would life have to get before you considered suicide?*

Q *Can you foresee a time when it would be considered normal to end your life prematurely?*

Q *Why do you think we are so quick to 'put an animal out of its misery' and yet would not think of doing the same for another human being?*

Q *Why do you think creative people are more likely to kill themselves than those of a more pragmatic nature?*

Q *If you were the only person left in the world after a terrible natural catastrophe, would you kill yourself or live alone for forty years and die of natural causes?*

' on fortune-telling '

Every year on a summer afternoon I dress up as the great
gypsy fortune-teller, Madame Lucasta, and pitch a tent
on the village green, in readiness for our church fête. I
read hands, I tell fortunes, and I take it all very seriously
indeed. In fact, so seriously that I spend at least a fortnight
revising my technique. It's not just a question of knowing
where the various lines are – of heart, head, life and fate
and their various tributaries – and what each intersec-
tion means. I also have to observe the 'mounts', the natural contours of the hand named after the planets, and take
account of the shape of the hand as a whole, the length and
thickness of the fingers, the state of the fingernails. The
truth is, I don't believe a word of it. So why is it that after
seven minutes with a stranger I feel I know them better
than after three hours talking to a neighbour at a dinner
party?

The other day I hit upon the answer. We all have an
unconscious filing system for everything we think and
observe. I love that fact. Even the thoughts I had earlier
in the morning as I phoned various friends have already
got happily logged into my memory, not merely into the

files labelled 'Trish, Louisa, Antonia and Kate', but also those labelled, 'Money, love, children, domestic arrangements' – and indeed as many files as the subjects we touched on. A human being's mind is so delightfully supple: it did all this without my even being conscious of it! The one aspect of ourselves which serves as an obstacle to this miraculous piece of filing is consciousness. If I'd been told, 'Be aware of all your conversations and begin logging them for an essay at a future date', I would be so busy trying to remember that I wouldn't be listening to what was being said, yet now as I look back, not just the content is still with me, but more importantly the *mood* of each conversation. If my husband asked me this evening, 'How was Trish?' I wouldn't just repeat everything she had told me, but produce a magic summary as well.

So when I am reading a hand my conscious mind is being taken care of. I've been given a task: where are these lines intersecting? Where are the breaks in this person's health? What does it mean when the Mount of Mercury is pronounced? And I thereby allow my unconscious to let rip: all that filing over so many years is paying dividends.

Human beings are brilliant at picking up clues as to what someone else is like. Within moments we can guess so much from the clothes people wear, the way they walk, talk, sit, smile, carry themselves: are they dreamy, observant, neurotic, angry, humorous, cocky, self-effacing, kind, needy? We don't *consciously* observe these things, there's simply too much data, but *unconsciously* we are comparing a particular look about the mouth with hundreds of others who also have that particular look, and, when summoned, we can even interpret what it might mean. And if we're so clever when we observe at a distance, think how intimate the act is of holding someone else's hand in our own.

The trick of fortune-telling is to relax. Here I am, their hand in mine. This is a hand which writes, paints, makes things, spreads butter on toast, touches other people, combs hair, brushes teeth, scratches an itch: for seven minutes this hand is here with me! And as I run my own fingers along the palm of the hand, the hand suddenly begins to belong to a person. I find myself telling them what the lines mean, yet simultaneously letting the subliminal be master. What I tell them bewitches both of us. It's like remembering a dream in the middle of the day.

What I'm talking about, let's face it, is intuition. It's the reason why no computer will ever be as clever as we are. Fortune-telling is akin to painting. In fact, it's akin to anything creative. It's about recognising the subtlest shades of colour in another human being and bringing them somehow into a coherent whole.

But, you might say, it's all very well being able to make a quick assessment of character, but what can fortune-tellers know about the future? The answer is: nothing much. Yet I'm certain that different characters attract different futures; or rather, if one person were to lose his leg in an accident, he might consider himself totally wretched, whereas another might consider himself fortunate to be alive. The Delphic Oracle in Greece, the Mecca of the ancient world for anyone who wanted to know his future, was clever at deflecting direct questions. So if I were asked the question, 'Will I be happy?' I might answer, 'As happy as you can be'. It's a sort of trick, I'm afraid, but a little true nonetheless. The future, like the present, is above all an attitude of mind.

food for thought

Q *Have you ever had your fortune told? Were you convinced by your fortune-teller that she had something valuable to say?*

Q *Why do you think fortune-tellers (at least those who read hands at church fetes) are most often women?*

Q *Would you say you were naturally intuitive about people?*

Q *Are you intuitive about your partner?*

Q *Do you agree that good fortune is above all a habit of mind?*

Q *Are you more likely to be dismissive of fortune-tellers than to be anxious about what they might say?*

' on jock '

I first met Jock about twenty years ago, when he used to knock at my door every week and ask if I had any odd jobs that needed doing. He was a Scot in his mid-fifties, with a slightly desperate look about him. I am a sucker for desperate looks – I'll do anything for anyone who looks me in the eye with an expression which says, 'Please, you're my only hope.' So I employed him to whitewash my kitchen, and for a long time I got a new coat of paint in there every three weeks or so.

I knew he drank, I knew he got into brawls, I knew he used to be a traveller with the gypsies. He was always on the edge of financial ruin, and one day he knocked on my door to tell me that his landlady had chucked him out and he'd be living in the park from now on. To find oneself at the crossroads of someone else's life is both alarming and invigorating. I took him to Housing, who were, at first, unhelpful. As a single man he would be at the bottom of any list, there was nothing they could do. Jock did very well. He told the young woman not to worry, he was quite happy on a bench, he'd lived on a bench for years and no harm had come to him. All he needed was a blanket. Could she provide an old blanket? And that desperate look of his was just too much for her. She found him a place in protected accommodation, where everyone else was twenty years older than he was but at least he'd have a roof over his head.

When I had children, Jock was still whitewashing our kitchen. I was exhausted: five sons, no garden – a bad recipe. So one day I sent him out, with the two youngest in their double pushchair, to push them round the park, and this was how he came to be part of my family. He adored my boys, and the boys adored him. He bought them sweets and sang them songs from the Highlands; as they grew older, he taught them about horse racing, gambling and cards. He also knows about birds, and can recognise every birdsong. We live in the country now, and he comes to visit so often that friends think he's the boys' grandfather.

Jock is seventy-seven now and going strong. He smokes three or four packs of cigarettes a day and when he's in town spends about ten hours a day in the pub – there's only one local which hasn't excluded him for bad behaviour, though when he's here with us he's never drunk a drop. His rent, including all bills, costs £10 a week – those with savings, he tells me proudly, have to pay £165 a week for the same deal! He hasn't paid tax since the 1950s, but recently he got a lump sum of £19,000 from a pension fund he'd contributed to when he was a college gardener all those years ago. As a consequence, he's drinking and gambling more than ever, but still thinks it too extravagant to buy himself decent clothes or a good TV.

Jock is as observant as he is blind, as placid as he is

angry, as much part of our lives as he is part of a very different kind of life. He never married, he never belonged to the 'system', which is probably why we all have such affection for him: he's the one that got away, the one that wasn't properly socialised. Those on the left might argue that he hasn't been given sufficient opportunities; those on the right that he's a scrounger. I can only rejoice that this society thus far has somehow accommodated him, and let him be who he is. Too much concern, too much control would turn us into a kind of Sweden, a perfectly functioning society without sufficient air. The world needs Jocks as it needs doctors and construction workers. Jock lives out that part of me that couldn't care less what everyone else thinks, that enjoys the moment, that has no truck with self-pitying introspection. Other people's lives make us who we are, and thank God for them.

food for thought

Q *Have you ever wanted to run away from your life and be a tramp?*

Q *Do you think that we as a country should take better care of our homeless, even if they've brought it upon themselves?*

Q *Was I wrong to let Jock push my children round the park, seeing as his CV wasn't exactly sparkling?*

Q *Do you think that those who have not paid into a pension scheme on a regular basis should have a significantly worse standard of living (perhaps a bedsit with shared bathroom and kitchen facilities) than those who have?*

Q *Do you think that what I feel about Jock is pure sentiment and that we should all aim to live in a society where there are no Jocks left?*

Q *Were your feelings on reading about Jock more those of shock (that I let him babysit for my children and have him stay in my house), anger (that his present standard of living is the same as those who have saved for their retirement), or appreciation (that men like Jock can have a good and meaningful life)? Or concern (that society hadn't looked after him well enough)?*

Q *When a stranger knocks at your door, how suspicious are you?*

Q *Have you had a bad experience as a consequence of trusting a stranger too much?*

Q *When your partner was a stranger, how long did it take before you began to trust him/her?*

‛ on being locked in the lavatory ’

When I was a child, between the ages of about nine and eleven, my brother used to lock me in the lavatory – as we called it in those days; even now, when I hear the word, these memories come flooding back. And, surprisingly, they are good ones.

When my brother, older than me by three years, had a friend over to play, he would send me into the lavatory, barely having to raise his voice. The friend would watch, mightily impressed by my brother's authority and my obedience, while he solemnly took the key from the inside and locked me in. This would be at about eleven in the morning and I would stay there till he released me for lunch; he didn't bother with me in the afternoon. I never told anyone, my brother and I never referred to it, though in 'real life' we got on quite well, and it never even occurred to me to smuggle in any comics. And it certainly never crossed my mind that I could escape from my little prison. I could so easily have clambered on to the loo and let myself out of the window, had I had any initiative whatsoever. But perhaps I felt, somehow, that that would have spoiled the game, even though it was never spelled out that a game was what this was, for both of us.

When my brother first locked me in, it took me a while to get into my stride. I didn't wonder how long I'd be cooped up in there, nor why he'd done it. Nor did I plot revenge. It was more a sort of looking around and wondering what to do next. At first it seemed as if the place were devoid of entertainment. Nowadays, of course, people stack their loos with books just in case, but our family took no such precautions. The sum total of reading matter was the back of bottles of Harpic and disinfectant. And then I found the carcass of a dead fly on the windowsill. Project Lavatory had begun.

I had never looked at a dead fly before, and it suddenly seemed to me to be the most extraordinary cohabitant in the world. We were reading *The Hobbit* at school, but this was much more interesting because it was real. How did its wings come to be like that? Its wiry black legs, its alien, spooky mouth, its enormous eyes – why were they like that? Imagine how awful it would be if flies were the size of dogs. Why did I think it was so ugly? No one had told me that a fly was ugly – or beautiful, for that matter. So did that mean that it was *really* ugly because I had noticed it for myself rather than just being told that it was? What did 'ugly' mean, anyway? Was a human being any less ugly?

So I was able to look in the mirror to check. On a scale of 1 to 10 it seemed to me that human beings were hideous too. If a fly scored one out of ten, did I merit more than three? How did we ever imagine that any of our species deserved that word, 'beautiful'? A dog's black, wet nose let him down; a cat, well a cat certainly scored higher than a dog with its green eyes, sleek fur, and fine deportment. But how was I judging these things? By what criterion? As I happened to be a human being, why did I not immediately pronounce mankind the most beautiful?

Then I sat down on the loo seat to examine not a mere reflection but the real thing: my body. What was this thing called 'skin'? I noticed, for the first time in my life, that there were little blonde hairs growing out of tiny holes. They could never have been enough to keep a human being warm. Humans would always have needed to wear clothes. But why did our hairy ancestor first decide to put on clothes? Was he suddenly too cold? Did the clothes then rub against his fur and cause him to lose it? And are any other animals ashamed of their nakedness like we are? What is shame for?

From flies and bodies I moved to the reading material: the ingredients of lavatory cleaners. These too I found mesmerising. I decided to recite them as if they were Shakespeare, or pretend they were a foreign language. I even learnt them off by heart, and even now can recite the ingredients in a bottle of TCP (Trichlorophenylmethyli-odosalicyl – try that as Shakespeare, or add an accent and see if you can make it sound like a foreign language). Who made up these names? Who makes up any language? The cleverest of the tribe? Was there ever a time early on in a language when grammar was completely regular? Because it's only common verbs which *are* irregular, as though they get irregular from being used too much. So, was there ever a time when people said 'standed' for 'stood' or 'seed' for 'saw'? You get the idea. One and a half hours passed by in a jiffy.

Nowadays, of course, children are never given that time. We don't give our children the chance to become an 'I', to feel that they can think anything on their own. We are indoctrinated from cradle to grave, by parents, teachers, our own peers. We have become totally used to being passive: a clever, or not-so-clever, receptacle of knowledge. We use our 'selves' to react, rebel or conform, but rarely have either the time or energy to merely think, purely and abstractly, about anything at all. So thank you, dear brother, for those many pleasurable, even enlightening hours in the lavatory. Thank you!

food for thought

Q *If you were locked in the lavatory for an hour and a half with nothing to do, what would you find yourself thinking about?*

Q *What do you think of the word 'lavatory'?*

Q *Do you ever worry that our present generation will be less thoughtful than those in the past, simply because there is no longer the quiet, empty space in which to reflect?*

Q *Some people like to read when sitting on the lavatory. Why do you think this is?*

Q *How claustrophobic would you feel if you were locked in a small room?*

❛ on violence ❜

The other day I found myself gripped by a programme on daytime TV. A quiz team was being asked to agree on what would be worst for a child:

(a) A diet of junk food, morning till night
(b) Twelve hours a day watching TV or playing computer games
(c) Being regularly smacked

The answer came back: 'Smacking is violence. No child should ever be smacked. Being regularly smacked would damage you for life.'

Funnily enough, when I was a child I would be smacked for exactly the (a) and (b) sorts of crime: raiding the larder for crisps before lunch, or sneaking down to watch TV after lights-out. I remember the sensation of being smacked like it was yesterday. It was extremely painful and shocking. Thwack! Just one smack, over my clothes, never naked flesh. After about twenty seconds the shock waves would subside and I would run up to the sanctuary of my bedroom to nurse my pride.

When I was a child we were all smacked by our mothers; that was the punishment of the day, as it were. In fact, so normal was it, that we felt sorry for children who had more subtle punishments. I remember once stealing sweets with a friend from my mother's cache on top of the tallboy in her bedroom. She smacked me, but not the friend. My friend's mother didn't believe in smacking, and she had to miss a birthday party the following Saturday afternoon instead. As I look back on this episode, does it seem to me that my friend's punishment was more humane or less damaging than my own? At the time I felt that her mother was obviously ten times stricter than mine, and I'd had far the easier time of it. Do I agree now with my first assessment, aged six and a half? Yes, but, because smacking at that time was normal, we all knew what 'smack' meant, what its currency was. Nowadays smacking is always 'violent'. So what does it mean to be violent?

The curious thing about violence is that it has two characteristics. Firstly, it is about physical force being applied to a body, and second – and this is the more interesting aspect – that it is somehow out of control. Why we outlaw it, why we have, as a culture, zero tolerance of it, is this second aspect. We are frightened of human beings who are out of control. But was my mother out of control when she smacked me? Absolutely not. Ironically, she would smack me to impose a certain order in life – this is what happens to you, darling, when you step out of line. So let's look at the other aspect of violence: physical force, the causing of *real* pain.

What is it about the deliberate infliction of pain on another human being that makes it an *absolute* wrong?

What about the words we use against a child who has done something she shouldn't have? My mother would have shouted at me, 'How *dare* you take sweets without asking!' She would have been angry – and anger is, after all, a loss of control, and therefore frightening – yet I would not only have understood her anger but thought it justified.

But what about my friend's mother? I'm sure she didn't lose control when she reprimanded her child as they drove back home together that afternoon. What if she had said to her, not in anger, but cool and firm, something along the lines of, 'You're nothing more than a common thief. I am so ashamed of you. And you're not going to go to the party on Saturday. You'll be spending the afternoon in your bedroom instead.'

Oh, the dreary heaviness of it! The trouble with punishments which aren't physical is that they eat into time. Rather like prison, time becomes your punishment; 'doing time', they say. Is it really true that this time-wasting we impose on the modern child is salutary in a way that the occasional thwack I received as a child wasn't?

Perhaps we're worried that if we allow smacking back into the child-rearing repertoire we will be condoning other forms of violence in the home, and it's better to have zero tolerance from day one. 'If my partner ever laid a hand on me that would be the end of our marriage,' my girlfriends tell me, and one friend even wants to take her ex-partner to court for hitting her once twelve years ago – no blood, no bruising even, but it was the 'insult' of it.

So I shall come clean. I have slapped both of my husbands once, and both times it felt really good and profoundly cathartic. In both cases, there was simply too much to say in too short a time, and I needed to express it. Words are the ideal, always, but when they remain unheard how is it possible to breathe, even? That energy has to escape, somehow.

Violence is ultimately an act of communication, and what is being communicated is unhappiness, disappointment, a sense of injustice. Articulacy is the key to preventing it. If we were able to recognise why we're feeling upset and put it into words, and someone else is then able to respond to those words, domestic abuse would be a thing of the past.

My mother believed that children should be trained rather than reasoned with. I think our modern tendency to explain why something is wrong, rather than just punish a child, is the correct and civilised one. But if I have a reader who believes that violence is *never* justified, and my resorting to violence in my marriage was a direct consequence of the violence I received at my mother's hand, I would like to ask that reader's advice about the following episode, when I was a mother myself.

My eldest son was a year old. He had a godmother, an aunt of mine whom I totally adored. I saw her as the perfect mother, all suet puddings and apple crumble, and we were staying with her for the weekend. As usual, my son made a beeline for the electric sockets, putting his fingers into them and then crying out when he got an electric shock. I laughed. 'He'll learn one day!' I said, shrugging my shoulders. My aunt was appalled. 'Do you want your child to be dead?' she said, gathering him up in her arms.

My aunt, my good, kindly, gentle aunt, mother of all mothers, grandmother of all grandmothers, then proceeded to take down my son's nappy and wallop him three times. Thwack! Thwack! Thwack! My dear baby boy, puce and trembling, cried fulsomely for a full ten minutes.

'He'll never do that again,' she said, calmly.

And he never did.

food for thought

Q *Violence is never desirable, but is it always wrong?*

Q *Sadism and masochism are sexual fantasies shared among supposedly mentally healthy adults. Can you understand why?*

Q *Do you enjoy violence in books or films?*

Q *Do you believe that smacking is violent?*

Q *Do you feel now that you were treated violently as a child?*

Q *How would you feel if your partner slapped you, if you immediately understood why – for example if you had bought yourself a smart new car on the joint account when money was tight?*

' on three made-up words '

The way language connects with reality is one of the most enjoyable and elusive philosophical problems in the world. How and why does language work so well? What is the relationship between a word and a thing? Is a language more than the sum of its words? What emotions do we know and recognise but which so far seem to be unnamed?

Well, there is one particular emotion that I totally despise but cannot help; and it is shared by my husband and sister and several of those I asked in church this morning, particularly the men. When expected to do something, every cell in our body craves to do the opposite.

A feeling so universal should have a name. I want to suggest three new verbs: oppi-think, which is to think the opposite of what you're supposed to think, but keep it quiet and certainly not act upon it, oppi-ject, which is the immediate and verbal contradiction of any suggestion put to you, and oppi-fact, which means to actually *carry out* something contrary to advice. There might even be such a thing as an *oppi-thought,* an *oppi-jection,* and an *oppi-faction.* The main point about these feelings is that *there is absolutely nothing logical about them*. Revolutionaries might have reason on their side, rebellions might actually be *caused* by bad leadership. But what I'm talking about are thoughts, words and actions which have no other basis for their existence but their being the *opposite* of another mode of behaviour which has been recommended.

One of the last things my mother ever said to me was, 'Darling, you have spent your life rebelling against any suggestion I have ever made to you.' I said to her, 'Yes, I have,' and felt I had never loved her more. Luckily, she had recommended a life of drugs, parties and leaving school the moment it was legal. I rebelled all right. I wanted to enter a nunnery and taught myself Greek under the bedclothes.

The depth and passion of my various *oppi-factions* beggars belief. During my Finals at Cambridge the requirement to do the very opposite of what I was supposed to be doing – an exam that mattered very much – was so great that I collared the adjudicator and in a private room tried to explain the unforeseen and powerful emotion with which I had suddenly been possessed. No one got married in those days, so I did the moment I graduated; posh girls and classicists didn't train to become probation officers, so I did; people were waiting to establish their careers before starting their families, so I had three boys on the trot. When the nurses told me to lay my new-born baby on his tummy, I laid him on his back; when they told me to lay baby number two on his back, I laid him on his tummy. When there are health scares, I do the opposite of what they tell me, *I just can't help it*. When we were told to avoid eating beef, we had steak every night; when we were told not to eat eggs, never have we eaten more omelettes. I am not proud of these facts, I am just quietly observing them. Can I really put it all down to having a bossy mother?

Yet I'm not bossy, and my sons, who on the face of it don't seem to be any different from anyone else, have all experienced the urge to deface paintings, or throw themselves under trains or off cliffs, or shout out in the middle of an important religious ceremony. And no, I don't think this is some rogue gene I happen to have passed on. To a greater or lesser extent this entirely irrational emotion is shared by all of us. God help us if we could attach thought bubbles to our oppi-thinking heads at the most solemn occasions. Luckily we rarely share our oppi-thoughts – which is why comedy works so well and we can experience a delightful release in tension – but there is an arena in which we oppi-ject and oppi-fact all the time: marriage, or when we have lived with someone else for a long time.

The other day my sister described to me the terrible quandary she found herself in when her husband told her, in just a very slightly know-it-all tone, or perhaps, simply, a 'helpful' tone (which is the same thing) to avoid the A27 because of an almighty traffic jam. Every part of her cried out to get on that road straightaway, but rationally she knew she didn't want to spend the morning in traffic. What was she to do?

Likewise, for fourteen years we have had twenty tons of topsoil dumped in our drive in November, which looks a sight and makes parking difficult. Our house is a converted barn, and back then, it's true, our two acres of land were a field – no trees, no flowers, nothing to ease the eye, and under an inch of soil there was pure chalk. Since then my husband has performed great earthworks: we have hedges, ditches, terraces, copses, and have planted everything from roses to rhubarb. In fact, he has created a wonderful garden, so wonderful that a friend of mine, a landscape gardener, thought the garden had been *inherited*, not made, and had simply been neglected over time. 'This garden must have been simply amazing in its heyday,' she said. Both Mark and I were delighted.

Yet I confess to a niggling part in me which hopes we might be let off the delivery of earth and allowed some time simply to take stock of his creation, and every year I begin a sentence in my most tactful and dulcet tones something along the lines, 'You have made the most magnificent garden, but what if this year . . .' I watch every fibre in his body stand to attention. 'You've reminded me I need to make an order,' he says. Nowadays all I can do is laugh and learn. Next year, I shall put in an order for a large vegetable patch, and finally the drive might be clear.

I find it very curious that psychologists and philosophers are always looking for the *reasons* for things. Perhaps there's a marital therapist reading this now who thinks, 'Well, *their* marriage isn't going to last very long! I detect a huge anger!'

Yet, speaking from experience, oppi-thinking, oppi-jecting and oppi-facting have *nothing to do with anything*, except, perhaps, some sort of deep desire for autonomy, a plea to escape a description of ourselves which just falls in with whatever is afoot.

It always amuses me when psychologists are brought

in to comment on some oppi-faction or other. Perhaps the man who recently defaced the Rothko really did have a proper reason: he had a rather curious slogan which he imagined would increase the painting's value, rather than decrease it. But if my son had defaced the painting, for the simple reason that he could, that it was possible . . . why do most psychologists *not allow that as a possible explanation*? Why do psychologists hate the idea of a 'spirit which blows where it will'?

I wonder whether there's ever been some serious scientific research into the subject of oppi-faction, and, if it was discovered that it was a real phenomenon, how it would shape future public health warnings. In the middle of the night I woke up with the idea of a screenplay for a public information film about drug addiction which went something like this:

A beautiful estate in South America; behind vast locked gates a drug baron is lying on a lilo in a marble-lined swimming-pool. But despite the happy chatter of the luscious women and children nearby, it's obvious that the drug baron is in pensive mood.

VOICEOVER: Antonio might seem to have everything. Women who love him, a beautiful house and healthy children. But profits have been down this year. There are fewer addicts than ever before, and his wife is expecting a baby.

Close-up of pregnant wife, patting her bump anxiously.

Antonio wants to send his son to Eton, the finest school in all England, but he's worried about how he's going to pay those school fees. Give the little lad a chance. Say yes to a pusher near you.

Would it work, I wonder?

food for thought

Q *What are your personal experiences of needing to do the opposite of something suggested to you?*

Q *Why do you think reason is so often powerless?*

Q *Why do so many people enjoy sports where there is a very real chance of death or serious injury?*

Q *Can you think of an example when your partner contradicts you for no reason, apart from the fact that he/she is contradicting you?*

Q *Do you think it's worth looking for courses of oppifaction, or is it just a part of being human?*

Q *What emotion have you experienced that you think needs a name? Can you make up a name?*

❛ on being a partner ❜

Last night my husband said to me, 'Don't touch me!'

I had just filled his brand new diesel-engined car with leaded petrol. He was not amused.

He sighed, said he couldn't believe how brain-dead I was, and went to sleep at 7p.m. I slept in another bedroom. And that was when it occurred to me that being a partner was rather like being a dancing partner: there was a skill to it, knowing just when to take a step forward, and a step back, knowing that this wasn't the right moment to remind him of his car crash on Christmas Eve.

I remember getting rather irritated with that book, *Men Are from Mars, Women Are from Venus*, which suggested that men need to spend some time in their caves and the best thing that women can do is to let them spend it. I read it at a time when I had five young children, and my God if I could have found a cave and spent the rest of my life there, that would have seemed the easier option.

I want to suggest something rather less extreme. There are people who both enjoy and need solitude, while others prefer company. Not only that, but in any particular couple at any particular time, there will be one with more energy to go out and do things, and one with less; there will be one who is more stressed and needs to offload stuff, one who is more receptive. There is no right, no wrong, no absolute; the rules in every relationship, like the steps in a dance, are to do with being aware of where the other person is at. And roles can be reversed overnight. Enjoy!

In both of my marriages I noticed a routine unfolding over the months and years. In the midst of life with young children, the best we could ever manage was a sort of pudding of a dance, a leaning into each other in mutual desperation. As we get older, and move beyond children, we are lighter and fleeter of foot. We are less zapped of energy, we play more: a game of Scrabble every evening after supper – unthinkable a few years ago. We often talk about inviting friends over to read plays with us; it hasn't happened yet, but what pleasure lies ahead.

When my son was about ten, he copied out for me some verses from the Bible. I had them framed, and they hang above my desk. They are about how to live well together. There is a time, says the author – for everything . . .

a time to break down, and a time to build up; a time to weep, and a time to laugh; a time to mourn, and a time to dance; a time to throw away stones, and a time to gather stones together; a time to embrace, and a time to refrain from embracing; a time to seek, and a time to lose; a time to keep, and a time to throw away; a time to tear, and a time to sew; a time to keep silence, and a time to speak; a time to love and a time to hate; a time for war, and a time for peace. (Ecclesiastes 3–4)

Last night saw a breakdown, a weeping, a refraining from embracing and was a time to keep silence. As I write this, the AA are draining my husband's car of contaminated petrol and tonight, who knows, might be a time for peace.

food for thought

Q *If your partner filled your new car up with the wrong fuel, how would you react?*

Q *If a partnership is like a dance, which one of you is the better dancer?*

Q *Do you think in general women are better at responding to the particular moods of men, or vice versa?*

Q *How long does it take each of you to unwind at the end of a busy day? Do you help or hinder the other from unwinding?*

Q *Relationships often suffer as a result of some terrible stress or sadness. People tend to dance alone, it seems, to different tunes. If you saw this happening to close friends of yours, what advice/words of comfort would you give them?*

‘ on vanity ’

When I was fourteen I believed that whatever characteristics were mine at sixteen would be with me for the rest of my life, but until that time I could more or less choose my character. I would lie in bed and ask myself, 'What kind of character makes you happy? And what kind of character makes you unhappy?' My answer to the first question was 'Goodness' because goodness is able to feed off and enjoy the happiness of other people; my answer to the second was 'Vanity'. If you are vain, you will only ever know loss. To be happy, you must avoid vanity at all costs.

Ah, those milestones! The first stretchmark (O, I reasoned, what is the pain of a stretchmark compared to the joy of a baby? Away, vanity!) The shock of the first grey hair (in a changing room in Laura Ashley I felt dizzy with shock and anxiety); the general sagginess of middle age. An article by Germaine Greer complained of feeling *invisible*: when our sexuality is spent, what is the point of us? Even my tea towel seems to agree. In its list of 'Ten rules for a happy marriage', it insists: 'Keep your figure, it's the only one you've got.'

On the radio the other day I heard a rather alarming

magazine item on French health visitors. After the birth of a baby, just like in Britain, they come round to visit a few times. But the object of attention is not the baby but its mother. How is your diet coming along? Are you doing your pelvic floor exercises? Are you having sex again, and if not, why not? Maternal exhaustion is no answer, I'm afraid. Your partner, you are warned, will be looking elsewhere if you don't satisfy him NOW!

So in France vanity is no longer vanity but a sort of wifely duty. Keep yourself in trim or he'll be gone, is the message. But isn't beauty meant to be skin deep? And what about those pretty girls who tell their partners, if you only love me because of the way I look, you can't really love me? Now, it really gets complicated.

I have two groups of friends: those who never set foot in a gym and will happily help themselves to an occasional cake; and those who diet and exercise as though their very life depended on it. These groups are suspicious of each other. Does either have the moral supremacy? There was once a time when I would have said, no question, be lazy! As I watch my body go down the spout, I'm not so sure. How much should I resist it? At what point does resisting the onset of old age seem sensible, and at what point does vanity rear its ugly (or conceivably its beautiful) head?

Then there is the equally thorny question of vanity in men. Do women like it, laugh at it, or loathe it? What if you found out that your lover had secretly been dyeing his eyebrows? (Does 'secretly' make it okay?) I once found the black hair dye of a boyfriend smudged over the pillows one Sunday morning. My reaction was to leap out of bed, barely say goodbye, and jump into the first bus that ran past his house. That affair was over pretty quickly. Should I have been more sympathetic? After all, prematurely greying hair will make men feel as anxious too; and they have balding pates and beer bellies to contend with.

Good looks, after a certain age, are not effortless. My husband bikes twenty-five miles a day to keep himself fit and lean; he cares about the clothes he wears, about whether something fits well. Would we want a man *not* to care? Yet a man who cares too obviously about the way he looks is as unattractive as a geek: intelligence and physical attractiveness should be worn lightly, or they cease to charm. For myself, looking in the mirror is a private affair, nowadays more for purposes of damage limitation than vanity. And I fear that however philosophical I am about growing old, the loss of whatever physical assets I had will irk me.

food for thought

Q *Do you consider yourself vain?*

Q *What worries you most about getting old: losing your looks, your health, or your life?*

Q *Do you think French health visitors are wise to concentrate their attention on the new mother rather than her baby?*

Q *Does it bother you that your partner's getting older too, or do you concentrate any anxieties you have on your own deterioration?*

Q *Do you feel that some vanity at least is a good thing?*

‘ on loneliness ’

I began to write my first novel when I was twenty-seven. It is about a man who goes to extreme lengths to communicate with his fellows. He cannot bear the fact that he inhabits a singular body and sits alone in it, that he can never know whether his experiences are shared by others or not. He spends twenty years of his life transcribing a piece of music into colour: his ambition is to find just one person, over the course of his lifetime, who can hear the music in the same way as he does. I was quite proud of myself at the time for writing a first novel which wasn't autobiographical. About fifteen years later I realised that it was absolutely about me.

My poor husband. It's not just that I want to know his every thought, I want to know how he thinks it. I want to know whether he thinks in fully formed sentences, half-baked sentences, visual pictures, or whether he experiences moods rather than thoughts, and, if moods, whether they are moods all of one colour or in different colours, and if different, whether the colours run into each other or not. For example, is it possible to be in a good mood and a bad mood at the same time? And do mood-thoughts count as thoughts or moods? And all this at the end of a hard day at work.

But I'm not just interested for dry, philosophical reasons: how thinking happens and all that. I need to know the answer because I need to know I'm not alone.

The awful truth is that the longer you live the harder it is not to feel lonely, a deep existential loneliness. Or perhaps I am peculiarly demanding: my mother used to have a ripe old time playing golf and bridge with the same band of friends she had as a teenager. I'm sure she didn't ask them, 'What exactly do you mean when you say you like that particular song? Whereabouts in your body are you experiencing the pleasure, exactly?' It was as though, by magic, they all seemed to know where everyone else was coming from.

But it occurs to me that as I grow older, as my sedimentary layers accrue and I become a wholer person, I am increasingly unlikely to come across people who have known me while those layers were actually being laid. For example, I have lived in West Sussex for twelve years; I moved here long after my first marriage was over and I am now, well and truly, 'the surgeon's wife'. People might say about me that I am open, friendly and easy to get along with; slightly eccentric, perhaps, occasionally unreliable and not particularly good at joining in. I am also known as the mother of lots of boys, and some must have guessed (though no one has quizzed me about it) that my first three have another father, because they have a different surname. But my former life is a closed book to them, and even if I were to describe a few of my adventures in my twenties and thirties, none of them lived by me while they were actually going on. Therefore, however much I tell people, if I were to rent the Hollywood Bowl and amuse (or bore) an audience of tens of thousands with stories of the things that have happened to me, however true and heartfelt my confessions, not a single person would know me. I would be known, rather, as an egoist with something to prove.

Because that's true, it amazes me how many people are zealous in keeping their privacy. I am zealous in getting shot of mine. I want to say, 'This is what it feels like to be a person. Here are both my good and bad instincts, these are the bits I know about myself, and these are the bits which remain a mystery – and which I enjoy, because they are a mystery. Is this what it is like for you?'

When I first moved here I was shocked at how lonely I was. I had to organise a bus for fifty-two old Cambridge friends to come down to visit me, I simply couldn't bear to have lost them all at one swipe. But even more than my friends (whom I could still phone or meet in London) I missed the neighbours, the local shopkeepers, the librarians, the market stall holders: all those people I hardly knew but who provided the fabric of my existence, who made me, in a way, *normal*. Without them, I felt myself falling apart, my sense of *me* fragmented.

So what will it be like when I am old? When my friends are too frail to visit me, and too deaf to hear me on the phone? If I require (as I do) totally close, open, subtle, generous friendships, what will I feel when a kind, young volunteer asks me if I had a good lunch? From this vantage point, the pain of that question is unbearable.

food for thought

Q *When has been the loneliest time of your life?*

Q *Am I unreasonable in my demands for closeness?*

Q *Would you say you are lonely now?*

Q *Is it important to you to chat to local people who do not count strictly as your 'friends'?*

Q *If you were the newly appointed Minister for the Elderly, what ideas would you have to prevent old people feeling lonely?*

Q *Is it enough for you to be on friendly terms with a lot of people and not to be particularly intimate with any of them?*

Q *Do you ever discuss your marriage/relationship with your friends?*

❛ on infidelity ❜

In 1973, when I was a girl of thirteen, my mother said to
me, 'Darling, I wish to give you some sound advice. It's
important you remain a virgin till you marry. No good man
wants soiled goods. But after you're married and have had
your children, take lovers if you want them. But you must
do so with absolute discretion, no one must ever know.'

When I was sixteen, my mother said to me, 'I've discovered that the rules are all inside out nowadays. You are to
have as many lovers as you can before you marry, though
the important thing is that no one finds out quite how
many or people will call you loose. But then, I'm afraid, you
are to remain totally faithful to your husband, even if he's
impotent. Goodness knows, I don't like this new way at all.
What will happen to the family? I predict divorce, divorce
and more divorce.'

When I was nineteen, my then first boyfriend intro-
duced me to his father, who gave me a book he had written
about his parents. They had loved each other with a very
deep love, yet both had taken other sexual partners; of the
same sex, as it happened. The book made sense to me completely. I love love. I am a romantic. To have pure love bat-

tle with mere sexual desire and for love to win, YES! That seemed a truth indeed.

I married my first boyfriend. Our hugely romantic notion was that one day we would live in a large house with an east wing and a west wing. We would live independently of each other and live passionate lives but meet every day for lunch to confess them. Until then, we were rather more practical about infidelity. We decided that the word 'fidelity' meant trust, and that our hearts would remain absolutely faithful to each other for ever. But bodies were bodies, weren't they? So, the rules were: when my husband was abroad for a period exceeding two weeks, he could have an affair providing (a) he had my permission in advance, and (b) the woman didn't live in England. My quid pro quo was that I should be allowed ten snogs per year and one two-week affair every other year providing that the geographical location of the aforesaid affair was Stoke Newington. Even now, the words 'Stoke Newington' quicken the heartbeat, and I feel a certain frisson, though I never actually met anyone who came from there.

When I was twenty-three, a year after my marriage, I was training to be a probation officer, and in those days part of our job description was to advise couples who were having difficulties in their relationship. My very first couple, what must they have thought of me? Twenty-three, looking more like eighteen, and they must have been in their mid-thirties. The wife could barely talk for tears; the husband sat there ashen-faced. He had been unfaithful to her: now she found she could never trust him again and wanted to divorce.

As trainee probation officers, we were expected to feel

'empathy'. I looked into the core of my very being and found none. What was their problem? Hadn't they realised that bodies were bodies and that it was human to feel desire and that sometimes it was impossible to resist? Had neither of them experienced feeling extremely hungry and being offered chocolate cake even if it's only half an hour till supper? I remember fumbling for words. I said, 'I'm afraid all I can see in this room is the absolute love that you have for each other. For either of you to turn your back on that love seems a tragedy.' I meant it. Love is all.

What went wrong with my first marriage was that we broke our own rules. My husband asked my permission while abroad for a short affair, but it so happened that the woman lived in London. After seven years and three children, I felt confident. I said, 'Okay, just this once.'

It wasn't. Forbidden fruit and all that, just an hour away. What is new and clean and fresh and far from the domestic tyranny of life proved irresistible. What happened to me then was the first real suffering I had ever known. Even now, I know that the demise of my first marriage was what joined me to the rest of the human race; up to that point, it was as though I had been effortlessly floating.

When I married a second time, three years later, my new husband said to me, 'Olivia, I shall be absolutely faithful to you, and you shall be absolutely faithful to me. Do you understand?'

I remember thinking, 'What, not even Stoke Newington?' and I felt a sensation of physically closing down, as if the world and all the possibilities within it was about to disappear for me – or rather, that I'd just been told I couldn't eat in restaurants any more, and could only eat at home. But of course I said yes.

A year later I was doing research on human sexuality and went to a series of lectures at the Cambridge theology faculty. Naturally, I was sceptical. But when the lecturer began, 'Sex is intrinsically meaningless', I thought, 'Of course it is, so what are you going to do about it?' and was all ears. For Catholics, marriage is a sacrament. Two people are joined together by God, and sex is what happens within that marriage. Only when there has been no sex within a marriage can that marriage be annulled; that's how important sex is. I am not a Catholic, but I was excited to discover that sex could theoretically be given any meaning at all: that sex can be sanctified, that the marriage bed can become a sanctuary, seems a wonder indeed.

Yet what does it mean when we desire a person we are not supposed to desire? What happens when it becomes more than a light-hearted fantasy? Is the desire to be unfaithful more than a physical restlessness? Perhaps there's more to infidelity than wanting to have sex with other people. Perhaps it's more akin to long-haul foreign travel and adventure, a need to escape the predictability of everyday life.

The trouble with marriage is that it can either be too intimate or not intimate enough. Close-range toilet habits do not hold the key to eroticism. Knowing how your partner thinks, knowing the contents of his/her mind, might not, on the face of it, make an evening in a particularly exciting prospect, while spending an hour perusing dating sites for fellow would-be travellers can be quite thrilling. There's someone tall, slim and mercurial out there looking for you;

or, if your mate doesn't happen to be your soulmate, there's someone out there who is.

Actually, if a soulmate is what you're after, how about making a new friend? Funnily enough, I would be ten times more jealous if my husband made a special 'friend' in whom he confided secrets that should be, by rights, my secrets. If it's an exotic body you're after . . . I've just begun the sentence and am weighed down by a sense of so-whatness. Okay, if it keeps the family together, if you'll go mad if it's not yours, if you're totally discreet, if you know what you're doing. Just remember how trite the whole business is, and be a little guilty, and a little ashamed.

I have now been married for eighteen years. It's a closed, traditional marriage, for which we had a blessing in a church. Weirdly, paradoxically, I see marriage as a room in which all things are possible, and I like it for that. I have never found another human being banal or boring for a moment; each of us can be prised open just a little more to reveal the extraordinary. The idea that no other body is mine but his makes me feel as though he is the last man in the world and I am the last woman: it's strangely sexy. In my book, fidelity works.

food for thought

Q *How important to you is absolute fidelity?*

Q *If a friend of yours told you that he / she was splitting up from his / her partner because of a single act of drunken infidelity, what would you advise them?*

Q *When was the last time you felt sexually jealous? Can you analyse the emotion?*

Q *How would you cope in an 'open' relationship?*

Q *What do you think of the sexual mores of those depicted in TV programmes such as* Upstairs, Downstairs *and* Parade's End? *Is our modern intolerance of infidelity a kind of moral progress, or rather dull?*

Q *Some of my friends argue that to confess to infidelity to their partners would double their original crime: you might ease your burden of guilt, but you make another person miserable. Do you agree with them?*

❛ on art ❜

I have always found art peculiarly difficult to make head or tail of. When I was eighteen I failed my Oxbridge general paper trying to answer the question, 'Is a forgery a work of art?' because I was still pondering the subject one hour into the exam, and to this day I've carried the question around with me, and make occasional attempts to answer it.

From time to time I've made a particular effort to get to grips with the subject. The time when it was most urgent to do so was when I was trying to impress my future husband. I was twenty, and about three months previously we'd split up, on his suggestion. I was miserable, but thanks to my impeccable upbringing I knew exactly what had to be done about it. Be Brilliant. Be Beautiful. Be with Someone Else.

So I went on a diet, had a new haircut, bought a sexy dress, flirted outrageously with anyone who was more handsome than the real object of my desire, and all that needed to be done was to master the history and philosophy of World Art. Everything was going perfectly to plan. My ex had been 'urgently' trying to see me for at least a month, but I'd refused – the golden rule is play it cool, the family motto – and finally I'd consented. We were to have lunch at the Royal Academy of Art in Piccadilly, and enjoy some new exhibition or other.

Luckily one of my housemates happened to be the World Expert on World Art, a man called James Malpas who to this day lectures at the Tate. I remember planting myself on his bed, sighing, pleading, 'James, you've got to teach me everything you know.' James was very obliging. I can't remember the name of the artist, but he told me a few biographical details, and why the artist was so esteemed. But as I left his room he told me something that I *do* remember. 'Olivia,' he said, 'I can't teach you how to respond to a work of art. You have to let the picture into you, somehow, you have to allow a work of art to take you somewhere. Be open to it!'

Well, I tried to follow the wise man's advice. But then, as now, I find it very difficult to follow; I am always anxious about *how* I am responding. I'm not happy with, 'all art is subjective, it's all a question of taste'. I feel there has to be something 'true' about art, which is why the question about forgery is such a tricky one. We have a gut feeling that forgery is bad, while art is good. But is that just superstition? After all, we have prints and lithographs, and we don't call them forgeries. Just as in print, in a paperback lies all the original intention and passion of its creator. And if someone argues that a forgery is always going to be 'second-rate' to an expert's eye, what if it were possible with modern technology to replicate *exactly* the colours used and even the thickness of the paint over every part of the surface, and indeed, what if this technology resulted in a new kind of art book – say, a box with ten paintings on *exactly* the canvas used by the original artist, so that it was quite impossible to tell them apart – what would be the difference between the original and the copy? This is where we really get superstitious. The artist himself has *touched* the brush which *touched* the painting – all his energy has gone into this very canvas and none other. Research has shown that people would be reluctant to wear Fred West's washed jumper because they believe his spirit still resides there. Do we believe in some medieval way that Picasso's spirit *actually* resides in his paintings, and that's why they're so expensive?

So if it's not its uniqueness which makes a painting 'true', what is it? What is it that an artist is trying to depict, or what is it that an artist *does* which makes his work 'true'? For what it's worth, I believe he depicts an 'essence' and asks a question; and it's that posing of the question which differentiates art from mere design or illustration. The question is an open one and by definition can never be answered, but can be re-visited for all time; and the essence is its quiddity, or what it is that makes a thing itself.

If I were teaching a class of children about art, I would hand out wooden frames, perhaps eighteen inches square, and say, 'Let's find out how much art there is in this room!' I would then encourage them to put these frames around anything they see, like their packed lunch or the coloured pencils on their desk. I would say, 'Look what a frame does! Now your lunch isn't your lunch any more, it's a picture. The frame makes us want to ask questions, it makes us interested. Who made the lunch? Who's going to eat the lunch? What are the shapes of the different kinds of food? What can we tell about the person who made the sandwiches and the person who is going to eat the sandwiches? What is the story behind the lunch?'

A frame (and it doesn't even have to be a real frame, merely a conceptual frame) pronounces that the object inside it requires a different kind of attention. Damien Hirst's shark in formaldehyde might have happily found a room in the National History Museum as 'A tiger shark caught in Hervey Bay, Australia'; but Hirst takes exactly the same object and puts it in an art gallery. Immediately, because art is about the universal and eternal, it becomes 'sharkness' or the 'essence of shark as man might meet it' and asks to be looked at in a different way. The idea in conceptual art is then to give the work a clever title, to make us think. So Hirst calls his shark-art, *The Physical Impossibility of Death in the Mind of Someone Living*. Perfect. We are made to think of our own mortality. Conceptual art is brilliant at revealing the concept behind art, at showing us how art works and what distinguishes it from photography (the threat of which made art redefine itself in the early twentieth century). It is, therefore, a kind of pictorial essay on the subject of art. But as art itself, of course it's not. Art belongs to a tradition which requires skill (the word 'ars' in Latin *means* skill), and even if that tradition has been waylaid for a hundred years or so, in its desire to set itself apart from the camera, does it really wish to divorce itself from the previous ten thousand years? And those children with their frames, though they had inadvertently revealed the nature of art, did so with no skill. Hence they weren't artists.

My real difficulty with art, however, is with abstract art. I can see from looking at my definition that some abstract art can undoubtedly be 'true' in the way that I want it to be. But I just can't get there, and the reason is personal.

Between the ages of ten and twelve I had an art master at school, called Mr Wolf, who was very keen on abstract art and keen to initiate us into its mysteries. Following my grandmother's advice – if you do not fear humiliation you will rule the world – I could throw myself into this world of self-expression, and did so. I rapidly became his favourite pupil, and he gave me my own studio, so convinced was he of my genius. He bought me brushes, canvases (some ten foot wide: he used to commission me to paint the backdrops for school plays, which is how I got my own studio in the first place.) He bought me the best paints: gouache, oils, watercolours, spray paints. He told me he would buy me anything I wanted, I just had to say.

Well, Mr Wolf, you made me incredibly happy. I loved being in that room. I have always been a sensualist: just the feeling of the brush in my hand gave me such pleasure, the weight of it, the extra weight as I dipped it into the paint, the feeling of stroking the canvas with it! I have always loved colour – even now if I spot a beautiful colour in a shop window or a flower bed, I have to cross the road to take a closer look. And how wonderful it was to feel that I was discovering new colours! I would mix and mix until a colour was so beautiful that I couldn't resist filling my brush with it. And this was how I carried on.

Now, I couldn't even sketch a dog. I had no interest in what anything in the world even looked like, let alone committing what I had 'seen' (in some mystical way) to paper. I had no interest in essence, or quiddity, or truth; only in pleasure.

The trouble I have with modern art is that it's very easy.

In fact, this is the kind of thing I might have done aged eleven. See if you can do it at home:

1. Buy yourself a large, good-quality canvas, some waxed card and some spray paints.
2. Practise with the colours you have chosen, and choose the two that you like the best and which mix the best.
3. Get in control of the spray can, trying it out on some newspaper; observe how you make a thinner, denser line, or a more 'sprayed' effect.
4. Make a 'wash' with diluted watercolour – a colour sympathetic to the spray paints you have chosen.
5. Have two glasses of wine (for adults only, children don't need it) and feel deeply relaxed. Put a spray can in each hand.
6. Start at the top of the canvas and pretend your left and your right hand are dancing together, mirroring each other, sometimes overlapping – so that the two colours mix – and sometimes standing alone.
7. When you reach the bottom of the canvas, look at what you've done. It will seem like a rather good and colourful design. To make 'art' out of it, fill a random space with a random other colour. To make this seem professional, use the waxed card as a stencil so the lines are sharp.
8. *Voilà!* Your friends will love this. They'll see something mysterious in the shape of the block of colour, particularly if you say that someone else painted it and it cost a small fortune. They will say, 'I see a bear!' or 'A Maltese cross, how amazing!'

Though Mr Wolf was entranced by my 'talent', my mother was less so. She would say, as I bought yet another painting home, 'Do you really call that art?' For a long time, she collected the paintings in a drawer in the bottom of the toy cupboard but when I was sixteen (and four years into painting 'still life' at my new school) she decided to clear out that cupboard, and we placed the paintings on my father's bonfire. I could have objected, I suppose. I remember feeling a great sadness, not because of the loss of the magic thing called 'art', but more, for the loss of my childhood.

food for thought

Q *When you go to an art gallery with a friend, how eager are you to talk intelligently about what you see?*

Q *What kind of art 'speaks' to you?*

Q *Why do you think art galleries are fuller than ever nowadays?*

Q *Does Tracey Emin's* My Bed *seem like 'art' to you? Do you think they make the bed when they put it into storage?*

Q *If I were to take an unborn baby in formaldehyde from the basement of the Alder Hey hospital, and give it the poignant title* Waste, *would that count as art, do you think?*

Q *How important is art to you?*

Q *How dependent do you think modern art is on the title artists give their work, and their own commentary on it?*

❛ on growing apart ❜

The other evening I was at a dinner party. I've always been useless at small talk, and seem to be getting worse as I get older, but even I wasn't expecting the conversation I was to have with my handsome, retired, gentle neighbour.

'So,' I said to him, as my opening gambit, 'what do you think the main building blocks of happiness are?'

'Football,' he ventured.

'No, no, surely not! The misery when your team loses can colour an entire weekend!'

'And the pleasure when they play well and win, nothing can touch it!' suggested my neighbour. 'So what makes you happy?'

'Living with people I love,' I said, which I could see sounded rather tame.

'I beg to disagree,' he replied. 'I haven't loved my wife for years,' he said, 'but I'm perfectly happy.'

'You can't be! How can you be happy living with someone you don't love?'

His wife was sitting opposite us: animated, younger than he was, good-looking.

'Of course you love her! If she were to die tomorrow you'd be wretched!'

'I dare say I'd remember her more fondly in death,' was his retort.

Why do couples grow apart? Why do couples get hitched in the first place? Perhaps the two questions are related.

People have very different reasons to 'commit' for a life-time. Nowadays, when I talk to young people, their reasons seem to me to be too sensible for words. 'Because I'm the right age to settle down. Because I want to have children. Because I don't want to be single. Because he/she can give me financial security.' Perhaps some of these modern couples are never properly together, so we cannot accuse them of growing apart. When I ask them, 'Whatever happened to falling in love?' they are ruthlessly dismissive. Falling in love is for teenagers, it's not real, it doesn't last; 'falling in love' is another way of saying 'having a crush on' – it's for kids only.

I've just been reading a book which tells me that people want their 'other half' to replicate patterns in their childhood. I could quite see how someone who associates cruelty with normality seeks the same normality in adult-hood. Then I tried to think how this might be true for me. And yes, I have one very real and wonderful memory of my childhood: the unconditional pleasure of having a friend over for the day. Sometimes we would put on a play for the grown-ups, sometimes we would invent our own language so the grown-ups didn't understand what we were talking about (I still remember the grammar sections!); we played Scrabble, tennis, watched TV together. The possibilities in any particular day seemed endless. When I got married, both times, I was looking for someone to play with.

Rather alarmingly, a chapter in the same book has the title, 'How to grow up at last'. I think I would die rather than be in a grown-up marriage. I'd rather we spent the evening in the kitchen throwing rubbish at each other than be civil, polite and grown-up. Fighting is passionate, you're in there together: in a real sense you are being absolutely true, both to yourselves and to each other. Growing apart happens when there is distance between you.

If I were a marital therapist I would have such fun. I would make my couple play draughts; they might even play draughts wearing each other's clothes. Or they could buy a couple of copies of a play about marriage – Noël Coward, Terence Rattigan – and act it out together! The trouble with therapy proper is that there is an awful heaviness about it. That line in American movies, 'We need to talk' makes me want to run out of the cinema. A fat person who goes to the nutritionist knows what's in store – you're eating too much of the wrong kind of food; and unhappily married people who've grown apart know exactly why they've grown apart – they've become boring to each other. They've become to each other, *someone I happen to live with*. They haven't been talking, or doing much else after lights out.

When there are no children involved and that's the way you feel about each other, then there seems scarcely any point in carrying on. But the tragedy is that children are so often the cause of couples losing sight of each other, and yet are simultaneously the reason why they need to stay together. It's exhausting bringing up a family, and that's no fault of anyone's. I used to wake up from a broken night barely able to speak a few words, let alone have a prop-er conversation. I would look at my watch and begin the countdown until I was allowed back into my bed, where I would read for fifteen minutes (the best part of the day by miles) before enjoying the bliss of dark and quiet. So how do you hang in there?

I used to insist that my husband and I had one genuine point of contact in any one day: sometimes just a meaningful look or a smile was enough. Which is, I think, the real reason why 'We need to talk' makes me want to run. Talking, when you're tired and have been at work all day, is often destructive. A hug says everything you need to say: no patting, just one firm embrace, strong, close, true. You hear and are heard all in one. Just perfect.

food for thought

Q *While I was on honeymoon in Pakistan, I was told again and again that the trouble with us Westerners is that we see marriage as a commodity like a car and we can simply get another when we've tired of it. 'We see marriages as a gift from God, a human being is very special. We cherish our marriages,' we were told. Can you see that there is a certain romance in an arranged marriage? If there is, do you not feel that there is at least the possibility of growing together after growing apart?*

Q *How good are you at psycho-talk? Is one of you better at it than the other?*

Q *In thirty years of marriage, I have never had one conversation about 'us'. My heart would nose-dive if my partner suddenly suggested we should talk about 'us'; I'd immediately think he was running off with his* girlfriend. Do you feel the same as me, or do you think there are advantages to having occasional state-of-the partnership summits?

Q *If I were your therapist and insisted you played a game with your partner, what would it be?*

Q *Are you competitive with each other? Do you think a certain amount of competition makes you closer or further apart?*

Q *If something annoys you about the other person would you tell them or put up with it? Why would you speak out or why would you keep quiet?*

‘ on being loved ’

When I was a child I was a great eavesdropper on adult conversations, which were obviously far more interesting than my own. I remember one in particular in which my mother told her assembled friends with a terrifying, absolute authority: 'In every marriage there is a lover and a beloved. It is infinitely better to be the beloved. The lover always gets hurt.'

My mother's opinion seems so dangerous and destructive that on no account must any couple discuss it, especially if it strikes a chord. For my own part, I cannot bear to agree with it. Instinctively, I want couples to love each other equally and for ever. I also want to suggest that to love is always the nobler thing, and to spend a whole lifetime merely being the object of other people's love is to live at half mast.

The other evening my husband and I were discussing what it feels like to be loved – our verdict was, we couldn't tell. When you're in the active role – loving – your entrails are stirred, your heart's warmed, you feel *moved*, but when you are simply *being* loved, unless you simultaneously feel love back, at best it feels like a cup of tea at the end of a hard day. In fact, if you don't love the person who's loving you, it can even feel smothering.

But when I relayed our conclusions to a friend as we were walking our dogs the following morning, she said, sternly, 'The thing is, Olivia, you have never known the feeling of not being loved. That's why you can speak so glibly.'

So I am now closing my eyes and trying to imagine the feeling of not being loved. I've never really cross-examined people as to whether they love me or not, I haven't even bothered to wonder whether they do or not. It seems to me that whether people love me or not has more to do with who they are, rather than who I am. Would they love me more, for example, if I were more or less successful? I tend to love those who are less successful. I am pleased for my friends' success, even to the extent of being proud of them, but my heart is moved by those who are going through a bad time. Does this mean, then, I should make sure everyone knows I'm going through a bad time in order to feel loved? Surely not!

I am now imagining what it would feel like if I had never known a parent's love, and my children despise me, and my partner is having an affair. For God's sake, you can all go to hell! It's time to run.

The good news is, however, that loving someone is something you can actually do, it's within your power. And loving someone feels really, really good. What's more, love is not a commodity, it's not subject to the rules of supply and demand with barely enough to go round. All one needs is a little time and imagination and *voilà*, the seeds of affection are sown. It's actually possible to increase the sum of human happiness for free.

So, Mum, I agree with you, the lover risks being hurt, he's laying his heart on the line. But what else can you do?

food for thought

Q *Can you think of a time when you felt loved? Can you describe it?*

Q *Would you prefer to think of yourself as the lover or the beloved?*

Q *Do you think we place too much emphasis on the importance of feeling loved?*

Q *If you could only know one experience, to love or to be loved, which would you choose?*

Q *Do you think it's possible for a child to feel too loved?*

Q *Do you think it's possible to love someone too much?*

' on fame '

Why does anyone want to be famous? Why trade in a delicious and free anonymity and be the centre of attention? The ambition nowadays of 70 per cent of schoolchildren is not to become a doctor or prime minister, or even a fireman. Their ambition is simply to be famous. We are supposed to be shocked and appalled at their shallowness. But I'm afraid I can't pull rank here. I remember the moment when I was fourteen years old when I realised nothing else mattered.

The lesson began innocuously enough. A teacher was ill and the headmistress was covering for her. She wanted us to think about our careers, she said. She handed out sheets with fourteen bullet points about what might be desirable in a career; she told us to list them in order of importance.

I only had to see the word 'fame' and I thought to myself, 'There's no competition' and wrote 'YES! NUMBER ONE!' in the margin next to the magic word.

When the headmistress asked to hear our results, she began, 'I trust no one here wants to be famous,' and everyone giggled, no one confessed. 'And what have you all put in the number one slot?' she continued. There was a veritable chorus: 'Helping other people,' they all said together. 'Yes,' she said, 'well done.'

Here was my second blow. Beside 'Helping other people' I had written number 13, only one ahead of 'Job security'. God help me! I was a bad person.

But the worst part of all of this for me was not that I was either bad or wrong but that I was doomed to be unhappy. I had always been interested in the question, 'What characteristics should a girl have in order to be happy?' and even kept a little notebook to reflect on the subject; and by then I knew this: girls who were happiest were those who were good and kind and shared their ration of sweets with a few close friends. Girls were unhappiest when they were too competitive and needed to be number one.

My only consolation was this: it was not too late to change. I gave myself two years to become good and rise above my desire to become famous.

Oh, the pain and boredom of it! On Wednesday afternoons all good schoolgirls would bake cakes to distribute at the local old folk's home. In my mind's eye I see a little troupe of clean, healthy girls with scraped-back hair in ponytails carrying baskets covered with gingham cloth. On one terrible occasion I joined them. They were all brilliant at it, chatting away as merrily as nightingales. I didn't know whether the old woman they sat me next to was a dud or I just couldn't do what they all seemed to do so easily – what do you say to someone with whom you have absolutely nothing in common? 'Ah,' these good girls told me, 'the old are wonderful! They have such characters! They are such fun to get to know!' I sighed heavily.

I failed equally on the fame front; I couldn't even comfort

myself that the fame I wanted was of a superior kind, as in famous psychologist or writer. No, I wanted to be a film star. I wanted a chauffeur and money to have beautiful clothes. I wanted to act in melodramatic films and have sex with directors on the casting couch. I wanted to have a red carpet unfurled before me and have people cheering me as I walked gracefully towards the premiere of my latest film.

Who was this 'I'? I wondered. Why was she so crass? How was I to be rid of her?

I asked my physics teacher, a concert pianist manqué with whom I was hopelessly in love. He was more than useless.

'Why don't you just let yourself be famous?' he suggested. 'What's your problem?'

'I don't want to be unhappy,' I told him.

'Why would you be unhappy? Perhaps you'd enjoy being famous.'

'Of course I would, for a year or two, but then what? How can you ever be real again when you've learnt to be unreal?'

By the sixth form my desire for fame was still burning and I was rapidly losing the battle to be good. I had an American uncle who lived in Hollywood and he was going to introduce me to some directors. Meanwhile, every year the lower sixth had to spend a week on a council estate in Camberwell to find out how privileged we were. Our headmistress told us it was our remit in life to help the poor and needy and give something back to society. Each one of us was billeted with a family for a week: we had to clean the flat for them and walk the children to school. We weren't even given a bedroom for the week, just a camp bed and a sleeping bag.

How I managed to wriggle out of that one I can't

remember, but I did. The girls came back to school full of it. Exhausting, but totally rewarding, was the verdict. I just thought: a lucky escape.

I got into Cambridge to read Classics and went to Hollywood in my year off. I had a figure like Barbie's and went to parties and had many adventures. The experience put me off any desire to be famous; in fact, I even gave up acting, my driving passion.

At the end of three years of Classics, I went to Leicester to study social work. And did it cross my mind that I wished to be the most famous probation officer who had ever lived? Oh yes! Of course it did.

food for thought

Q *Have you ever wanted to be famous?*

Q *Do you think famous people enjoy their fame, on the whole? If so, why?*

Q *As a social worker and probation officer, I have spoken at length to murderers, rapists and arsonists, and have never found it difficult to think of things to talk about. When I meet someone in the public eye, however, I find myself totally tongue-tied. Does this person actually want to talk about the article I've just read about her in the newspaper? Am I going to stoop to asking her where she likes to go on holiday? What would you talk to a famous person about?*

Q *Which famous person would you most like to meet, and why?*

Q *If your child told you that he wanted to be famous, what would you say? Would you encourage him or put him off?*

Q *Why do you think it might be difficult for a famous person to be happy?*

‛ on having needs ,

I have always been suspicious of the therapist's use of the
word 'needs'. A therapist asks you 'What are your needs?'
as though it's an open question; whereas the reply she's
looking for is something like, 'I need to be appreciated for
who I am. I need more time for myself. I need more sex.'

I have had half an hour of therapy in my whole life. The
NHS had actually paid for the whole hour – my marriage
had fallen apart and when my GP offered me six sessions
for free, my curiosity got the better of me and I went along.
Everything was going swimmingly. Being asked about
yourself is quite good fun (which is partly why I am writing
this book).

But then came the question. The therapist leant forward
and asked me earnestly, 'What are your needs?' I realised
immediately there were three kinds of answer I could give
her: the one she wanted; the theological and true answer,
which would have been something like 'God' or 'Meaning';
or one which would infuriate her. I knew the last would
make her hate me. I just couldn't resist it.

The second you sit down in the therapist's seat the implication is that you are a good person, misunderstood, and

vulnerable. For some reason, I can't bear anyone making any assumptions about me at all; or people can think what they like, as long as they keep it to themselves. So I told my therapist breezily, brightly, that I missed my former status. I told her that my father-in-law lived in a beautiful castle, and I missed the weekends we would spend there, when I was the chatelaine and I would entertain actors, writers and politicians. And now I was reduced to being a landlady and cooking for four students and being a single mother.

'Is that all you miss?' she said to me. 'Don't you miss your husband?'

'No,' I said, 'I don't.'

'Don't you miss the intimacy, the sex?'

'Oh no!' I said, happily.

'Well then,' she said, sternly. 'I think we're wasting our time, don't you?'

And that was that. I left her, tail between my legs.

The problem I have with 'having needs' is that I feel immediately cast as someone who is 'needy'. This assumption is intensely irritating. The therapist then implies that these 'needs' ought to be met, and that I should be blaming someone for not meeting them. *Poor you!* is the theme. Poor you who's living with someone who isn't looking after you properly! No wonder therapists (not Relate counsellors, who are great) do so much to hasten the demise of a marriage.

St Francis of Assisi wrote a wonderful prayer about having needs. It goes like this:

Dear Lord, grant that I may not so much seek to be

consoled, as to console, not so much to be understood, as to understand, to be loved, as to love. For it is in giving that we receive, and in forgiving that we are forgiven . . .'

There, much better! May the Force be with you, as they say in *Star Wars*.

food for thought

Q *If you had one need that could be met in the next five minutes, what would it be?*

Q *Who would you say had more 'needs', you or your partner?*

Q *Have you ever tried to change your behaviour to please your partner?*

Q *Has your partner ever tried to change their behaviour to please you?*

Q *Do you consider yourself more or less needy than the average person?*

Q *Helping others is often empowering, being helped sometimes humiliating. Why do you think this is?*

' on socialism '

Before I write this, I want to declare my cards. In any proper socialist revolution I would be the first on to the guillotine or in prison. In fact, I saw my cell only last year in Romania: a little grille at the door, no light, no bed to sleep on, with a chain and irons bolted to the floor ready to enclasp my ankles. I belong to the reviled bourgeoisie, and I wouldn't even get a job at the BBC.

But I am also aware of this wonderful concept 'confabulation', which means something like 'a rationalisation of something your gut wants or does not want'. So, for example, you might have a love affair *actually* because you fancy someone rotten and it's *really* sexy popping off to the seedy hotel down the road at lunchtimes; but when asked to 'rationalise' your behaviour you would talk about the failures of your partner, when you'd never even noticed your partner's failures until you met Mr/Ms Yummy Scrummy.

So what might be happening, when I resist socialism, is that my gut likes the status quo, because I have materially benefited from the status quo and I don't want to change my life even though it might be for the common good.

Kofi Annan used to say, 'There's enough in the world

for everyone's need, but not enough for everyone's greed', which I have definitely taken on board. Recently my older children have left home, and though they return for an occasional weekend, we could be accused of 'house hoarding', i.e. we have more bedrooms than we strictly need. It would even be quite easy to share this house with another family, a family in Britain that is presently homeless, or a refugee family. Yet even if I knew this sharing of property was being done all over the West, and even if I knew that as a consequence of this policy lives were being saved, I could not in all honesty wish for it.

Of course, there are socialists in this country – or they call themselves socialists – who would argue that I am talking about communism, whereas they are merely 'socialist'. I have difficulty knowing what this means – in fact, it might turn out that I'm one of these socialists after all: do I believe in the NHS? Yes! Do I believe in looking after the old and vulnerable? Yes! Do I believe in a good education for all, regardless of background? Yes, you bet I do, more passionately than anything. But for these 'socialist' projects where does the money come from? In our society, which is capitalist, not socialist, it comes from tax. So that those who pay it, and in particular those who give employment to other people, must be looked after too.

When I talk to my 'socialist' friends about their beliefs the truth is we agree about everything: our ends are the same, our means are different. They believe, correctly, that to make things fairer and increase social mobility we have to have better schools. To this end, they suggest, private schools should be abolished. They imagine that all those great teachers who are giving posh kids an unfair advantage would then find jobs in the state sector, and the state sector would be buoyed up no end. Not only that, but bossy middle-class parents would make sure that standards were raised because it was in their own interest.

What would really happen if private schools were abolished? The trouble is, change is exhausting and slow, and everyone would have to be going in the same direction. Teachers at private schools often love their subjects more than their pupils; they would show little tolerance to pupils who found their lessons boring. How long would they really last? But also, the ethos is very different.

I've read school reports from each sector: there is a tactful neutrality in the state sector which doesn't really put you in the picture about how well a pupil is doing. A teacher in the private sector is allowed to write 'she has produced nothing but utter crap this term. Is she going to too many parties, I wonder?' or conversely, she might be 'the best pupil I have taught in twenty years'.

There's also the encouragement of competition, and the determination to find what a pupil is good at – and not just good at, but better at than anyone else. In the state sector, the ideal is that everyone is good at everything. I know a headmistress of a primary school who's taken 'creative writing' out of her curriculum because it favours all those middle-class children who get read stories every night, while those phenomenally energetic parents who are creating 'free' schools in London, who would want *everyone* to learn to write a good story, are damned by egalitarians who would argue that creating a good school *ipso facto* means there is a less good school nearby, and that will never do.

A socialist believes in fairness, equality and looking

after the vulnerable in our society. If fairness means something like 'one law for all', and equality means a more generous 'equality of opportunity', and everyone wants to help the vulnerable, left and right, I would count myself as a socialist. But *real* socialists have a very different and more radical agenda.

Here is a question: If you could press a button, and everyone in the whole world lived on the same income in the same standard of housing, which turned out to be something the poorest in our society might inhabit, would you press it?' When I asked a socialist friend of mine, she didn't even pause to think. 'Yes of course I would,' she said.

This is where I differ from *real* socialists. I don't believe that human happiness is founded on the equal distribution of wealth. I believe happiness has more to do with human relationships, a sense of identity and being involved in something that *you do best*. I believe in the human spirit, and a society that allows us to be individuals rather than equals. I think *real* socialists concentrate their energies on the *material*: the having of things, equally and in common, and the human spirit is reduced to 'false consciousness'. Am I being too harsh here?

Here's another question to see if you're a real socialist or not. Imagine you are living on an average middle-class income. When it comes to your own children's education, which of these three arguments do you use?

(a) Of course I wish that the standard of a private education was available to all, I really, really wish it; but our local school is very poor and we're going to remortgage our house to send our children to the local private school.

(b) I don't believe in private education, and wouldn't even consider sending our children to a private school. However, we are spending £200 a week on tutors and hope to get our kids into Oxford or Cambridge.

(c) I despise those middle-class parents who pretend to be good socialists and then buy tutors to get their children into good universities. Children have got to learn to stand on their own feet. Three of our four children are now working in shops, but our fourth has got to uni on her own merit and we're proud of her.

The interesting question here – and these examples are all based on true stories – is that, though the third family is the most *socialist*, is it also thereby the most *moral*? Is it right that we should sacrifice our children's future for a *principle*. Is that the *ethical* thing to do?

If we sacrifice our own children, then the principle must indeed be very great. Socialism is about sharing the goods equally among members of a society. It is not about wanting equality of opportunity – who could not want that? – it is an *actual* sharing. The *real* socialist finds a homeless person and gives them their spare bedroom, and encourages others to do the same. That's what makes socialism incredibly difficult.

A final thought on the subject. People are always complaining that in a capitalist society there is a huge inequality of wealth – in fact, the difference between the richest and poorest is greater now than in Victorian times. (I feel rather like Ed Miliband here: there are the deserving rich, and the undeserving, parasitic rich.) But in socialist countries, there is an equivalent inequality of power. If we imagine the perfect socialist state – whereby the state owned the means of production and all property was held in common, a place where all could expect an equivalent education and health service and expect to live till a ripe old age, where there was enough for everyone's need but not enough for everyone's greed – a place not dissimilar to the concept of Christian heaven, 'where all our strivings cease': there would have to be a strong and powerful state, i.e. police force, to make sure no one such as myself was secretly hoarding rooms. Or how else might a *real* socialist's dream flourish?

food for thought

Q *Describe your perfect society in a perfect world. How would our values have to change?*

Q *Has the unfairness in our country ever made you angry?*

Q *If private schools were abolished, do you think standards would increase in our state schools? Why, or why not?*

Q *Are you good at genuinely sharing what you have with other people less fortunate than you?*

Q *Do you think that most socialists are more fired up by a love of humanity or a hatred of privilege?*

Q *If you are a committed socialist, and find yourself suddenly living in a country which reflects your values, but you have no power, would you be happy?*

‘ on jealousy ’

I have to confess, I don't really know the first thing about jealousy. It seems to be a phenomenally private emotion, so much so that, though it's possible for a gaggle of girlfriends to talk about how greedy they are, or how they fancy so-and-so something rotten, gaily bringing up confessions of jealousy simply does not happen.

I once tried to write a short story about an English teacher who was jealous of one of her pupils because her husband had once set eyes on the girl and had promptly fallen in love. She's angry with the girl, singles her out and ridicules her in front of the class, but the girl, of course, has no idea why.

I tried to get into the mindset of the teacher. In fact, it should have been quite easy for me: my first husband, whom I adored, one day announced that he was in love with someone else. But though my heart was broken and I felt utter despair, the woman herself had nothing to do with it. My love was based on intimacy, so I thought: I knew my husband through and through. Then suddenly I didn't know him any more. It was that loss of understanding, of possession, that upset me so. I had lost him.

I read *Othello*. I read other books about jealousy. But still I couldn't experience these feelings from the inside, and I knew, therefore, that I couldn't write convincingly, and I put the story aside.

Alain de Botton wrote a well-known book on status anxiety. I didn't buy it, because I am not sufficiently curious about people who are envious of others' status, or others' swimming pools, or tropical islands or what have you. It's so weird when an advertisement for a new car or new kitchen reads, 'Be the envy of your friends' as though you would *wish* to be the envy of anyone, particularly your friends. In Albania, when people began to build their own homes after the demise of communism, their final flourish would be an eye painted on the outside of the house to *avert* envy. This seems a far better way of going about things.

In a wonderful film called *Lourdes* there is the briefest of images of a young disabled woman looking up from her wheelchair towards her nurse, who is chatting away to another nurse about how on her next holiday she's going skiing in the Alps with some friends. The nurses laugh: one male, one female, both vigorous, full of health. They are mildly flirting with one another. We watch the disabled woman watching them, and the pain on her face is palpable. Is that what jealousy is like, a yearning to trade in one's lot and usurp another life?

Or perhaps, in a relationship, jealousy tells us something about the nature of love. Is love, by its nature, possessive? What is the difference between 'possessiveness' and 'fearing loss'? I know the second of those emotions, but I do not know the first. I delight in, rather than *own* my partner. When I hear how wickedly my husband flirts in the hospital where he works, with the nurses, doctors, cleaners, and even patients, I think, how life affirming is that! In a place all too familiar with suffering and death, what a breath of fresh air he must be. But if I knew there was a colleague with whom he was flirting, and it was not in his nature to flirt, it's not jealousy I would feel, an emotion which I've always imagined would be bitter, twisted, tight (though I might be wrong, and I'm not even sure who it's directed at), but *fear*: fear that he might fall in love with her, fear that I might lose him. Or perhaps that's just what jealousy is, fear of loss.

If I'm possessive at all, it's of my own individual journey. I remember as a child imagining I was in a Mini with a wrinkled map, but that was good enough for me, I would get exactly where I wanted to, and I didn't care how long it took. And if I spied a fellow traveller waving to me from the back of a Rolls-Royce, with her very own navigational team in the front, would I have wanted to trade places? Not on your life!

food for thought

Q *When you were a child, do you remember feeling jealous of someone? What was it they had that you wanted?*

Q *People tell me that sexual jealousy is the most powerful kind of all. Would you agree with them?*

Q *Apparently, people are happier if they have less money in real terms but greater parity in income with their friends. Has this proved to be the case with you?*

Q *What single possession of someone else's have you most coveted?*

Q *If you had to be someone else, who would you be?*

‘ on personal space ’

I am writing this at half past six in the morning, bang in the middle of my partner's personal space. The truth is, I would rather be sipping tea with him, or, even more ideally, persuading him to get back into bed because it's dark and cold out there. He'll be playing his violin, or watching snatches of sport on the TV, or reading the newspaper. I know he's already taken the dog out for a walk, because that's what he always does first. But I've learnt from past experience that there is simply no point in suddenly appearing in the doorway of whatever room he happens to be sitting in: he looks up, polite and far away. This man, for the moment at least, has nothing to do with me.

The sad thing about personal space is that the other partner can so easily be hurt by it. Personal space is, by its very definition, exclusive. It is also essential for one's mental well-being, and enjoyed, I believe, well or badly.

In less secular times people prayed. If a prayer is done well – these are the people I'm thinking about, these are the people I love, this is what I'm worrying about, this is what I'm grateful for (with a signing off, over to you, God) – what a stabilising and restorative activity it could be. Nowadays people tend to be less reflective, more concerned with the here and now, the material, more distracted by displacement activities. Partners demand personal space, and what do they do with it? They're on Facebook, logged on, checking sports scores, playing computer games. So the tragedy is, they're neither with their partners nor even with themselves.

Now I have acres of personal space, but there was a time when I had none at all, literally none, for days at a time. I used to be terrified of the dentist (we children weren't given anaesthetic), but things came to such a pass that I began to look forward to the privacy and passiveness of having a tooth filled, when I could lie at a very perfect tilt on a supremely comfortable chair, and be oblivious to the light or the fact that I was holding my mouth wide open. It felt like I was sinking back deep into the place I had originally come from: myself, myself only.

The car is a good place to be private. Here I can listen to speech, listen to music, or listen to myself. If I am anxious, or have to work something out, I have learnt always to take the third option, even if it would be so much easier to drown myself out with noise. A final observation: in the time that I count as my own I find myself either becoming a 'me' – rather like a newly laid screed for a floor, finding my own level and resting there – or an 'I', creative, dynamic, seeking change. It never bothers me which way the wind blows. I just go with it.

food for thought

Q *Are both of you aware of a need for personal space?*

Q *Are you tolerant of your partner's need for personal space?*

Q *Would you be more tolerant if your partner used that time in a way which you thought was beneficial, (i.e. sport, rest, reading) rather than just 'logging on' – or do both of you spend time 'logging on' and are therefore mutually tolerant?*

Q *If you were given a weekend off and could choose to spend that time either in solitude – reading, listening to music, walking – or with old friends, which would you choose?*

Q *If you were the partner staying at home and looking after the pets/children/house, would you rather your partner was recharging his/her batteries on some retreat, or partying with old mates of both sexes?*

Q *Are you good at being alone?*

Q *Do you sometimes get hurt by your partner's desire for personal space, even if you rationally understand it?*

Q *If your partner played a particular sport at weekends, would you consider taking up that sport because you felt left out sitting at home?*

‘ on saxons and gypsies ’

Last year we had a holiday in Transylvania and read a
wonderful book about the place, *Along the Enchanted Way*
by William Blacker, in which he describes his love for two
ravishing gypsy sisters. He, of course (as is the way with
travel writers), makes friends with everyone he meets,
but over the years he spent in the country was astounded
by the animosity between the Saxons (German-speakers
who settled in the country a thousand years ago) and the
gypsies, who've probably been around for even longer.
They could barely speak to each other, such was their
mutual loathing, but what intrigued me was that I
couldn't take sides, and the discovery that I myself, by
temperament, am half gypsy and half Saxon, and these
two sides of my character war continually in much the
same way.

The Saxons are a northern race, and take life seriously.
Their motto, in Transylvania at least, is 'Pray and work
hard'. They look after their houses, their clothes and their
crops. They know exactly what to plant, when. They know
how to scythe and store; they know how to sell their surplus. They are aspirational: they might even, with their

profits, put money aside so that they can send a son to medical school in Cluj.

The gypsies have no interest in the future: all is the pleasure and the music of the moment. They are employed as musicians at weddings. They are talented, charming, wonderful dancers, and neither work hard nor pray hard. In the evening they are to be found drinking, laughing and carousing. Each moment is sweet to them: every sunny day an invitation to take a picnic to the pastures. Their sexual habits are liberal, to say the least: they rejoice in their physicality, nature and music.

Thus presented, I imagine the majority of us would opt for life number two. One of my favourite passages in the Bible urges us to consider the lilies of the field: if God has clothed them so splendidly, won't He look after us too?

But what happens is this. In the cold winter months the gypsies simply run out of food. They, and their children, are at risk of starvation. The only option open to them is to beg. So they go to the houses of the Saxons and ask for food and money, and the Saxons can only give it to them. They are good Christians, after all. They can't let their fellow human beings die, can they? And the gypsies, after pleading poverty, holding out their babies swaddled in rags, spend the proceeds of their begging on a party. You can see why the Saxons feel such impotent rage.

I ask myself this. Deep down, am I a Saxon or a gypsy? I live as a gypsy. I love the minutiae of life, the smells of it, the texture of it. I even love stirring a wooden spoon in a cast-iron pan. I love this business of having a body, and the sensation of touching other bodies. I love not thinking about tomorrow.

But what if I lived in Transylvania and knew that every winter I had to knock on the Saxons' doors and endure their look of loathing and contempt? What if I knew that if I didn't change my ways my children were likely to *die*? I would be the first to stop dancing and start saving. I would become anxious and angry with those who weren't suffering as I was.

Now we have Germany bailing out Greece: the responsible one looking after the irresponsible one. If I were a German I would feel pure, unadulterated rage – my taxes supporting those feckless Greeks! But Greece, ah . . . the beauty that is Greece, the Aegean Sea, olives and feta cheese. Where would you want to live?

food for thought

Q *Are you more a Saxon or a gypsy by temperament?*

Q *If you were a Saxon in Transylvania, how would you cope with the gypsies begging at your door?*

Q *Would you like to become more gypsy/more Saxon or do you think you are about right?*

Q *Would you like to see your partner becoming more responsible or more carefree? What might you do to bring about that change?*

Q *Would you feel angry if you were German, or would you have the attitude, 'We're all fellow Europeans and should help each other out?'*

Q *What is your attitude towards having a decent pension when you retire? Do you see it as a priority, or do you feel that the future will take care of itself?*

〈 on infatuation 〉

At a dinner party the other day, our host asked us the following question: 'What would be most unbearable to you: that your partner should be physically unfaithful to you, just the once, for someone he or she didn't give a jot for; that your partner did care for someone, and saw them three or four times a week, for lunch, for a walk or a talk but no more; or that your partner became infatuated by someone, but had no intention of either revealing it to its object or of acting upon it, but lived obsessively with the idea of that *other*.'

According to the twelve of us, the least damaging to a marriage would be the first: mere physical infidelity, a one-off drunken episode which was immediately regretted. A close friendship would be more alarming, particularly one which happened while the absent partner was working. But we all considered – and I was surprised that the verdict was unanimous – that to live with someone suffering obsessive love – even if we knew it was ridiculous and when they got over it they'd think so too – was intolerable. A few weeks' grace might be permitted; any longer, the marriage itself was on the line.

If you're a teenager, obsessive love counts as a crush. It's par for the course. Teenage helplines warn you 'not to mistake intensity of feeling for intimacy', and you're 'on a roller coaster ride so hang on for dear life and enjoy it'. In adults, obsessive love is treated more seriously. It suddenly becomes a psychiatric problem: if you don't get help, you might even end up becoming a stalker. You suffer from obsessive-compulsive disorder. You have issues unresolved since your childhood. You're projecting all your unmet needs onto another person. In other words, you're suffering from a borderline mental illness.

What amuses me about infatuations is that the symptoms seem to have been the same in all cultures and for all time; it's how we interpret those symptoms that is culturally bound. Aristotle thought that this kind of passionate infatuation was caused by a 'boiling of blood around the heart'; and here are some case notes from the second century written by the Greek doctor, Galen:

> I was certain that her condition did not arise in the body, but rather in the soul – which was confirmed, as it happened, at the very moment I was visiting her. When someone came in from the theatre and announced that he had seen Pylades dancing, both the expression on her face and her colour changed. Seeing this, I placed my hand on her wrist and detected an uneven pulse, one that was suddenly irregular and agitated, a clear indication of a troubled spirit . . . thus I discovered that the woman was in love with Pylades, a fact confirmed by similar observations in the following days.

Good old Pylades, the George Clooney of his time.

In the tenth century, physicians in Arabia were treating the disease as equivalent to epilepsy. In a medical handbook especially written for travellers who might fall sick in a far-flung place where doctors were unavailable, *iskh* or 'passionate love' was the subject of Chapter 20, and lies in between a chapter on insomnia, frenzy and drunkenness, and one on sneezing and apoplexy. But when the book was translated into Latin and travelled west, *iskh* was promoted to become what we know as romantic love. Cupid and his arrows were suddenly in favour, and we had the courtly love of the medieval era, in which brave young knights fell in love with married women. A hundred years later such a love was seen as a disease again, and huge treatises were written on possible cures for the victim, my favourite being having a bath with seven rams' heads. At the end of the eighteenth century the Romantics appeared and a lot of young men committed suicide for their loved ones, and were commended for doing so. The Victorians had more self-control, but we in the twenty-first century seem rather ambivalent about whether passion is to be recommended or avoided. If my sons were never to fall in love in that way, never to pin all their hopes onto the object of their longing, I think something would be missing in their education. Yet what they'll learn from it is likely to be disillusion and pain.

The real danger and difficulty and sadness come, however, when the obsessive lover happens to be married. What if there's this man/woman at work who is utterly beautiful, and smiles at you in a certain way, and makes you feel young and full of the joys of spring? It's hardly your fault if you begin to obsess, but obsess you do till your home life becomes a mere cacophonous dream and your office a place of infinite possibility. Obsessive love is paramount to possession. The trouble is that though it's easy enough to ridicule or pity *everyone else* who's in this pathetic condition, if it's *you* who's possessed then the condition you're suffering from is far from a disease: you are in the throes of romantic love! And if you're not suffering from a bad conscience, life has taken on a new glow and you find yourself singing along to love songs on the radio. Enjoy, ah enjoy if you're single! You might even be in the first stages of a proper relationship. But if you're already committed to someone else, someone else you acknowledge you love very much, then the pain you are about to cause is pain indeed.

There is a line couples tell one another which is so painful that it would be easier to hear that you had to undergo an amputation. That line is: 'I love you, but I'm no longer in love with you.' As though the disease (fluttering heart/sickness/yearning) was more real than time and substance! Our culture allows that line to be delivered, in its high estimation of romantic love, but the ancients were right: romantic love is a kind of madness.

A psychiatrist friend of mine who's an expert on eating disorders tells me that obsessive love affects exactly the same part of the brain as anorexia: 'you will die if you carry on like this' has as little effect as 'you will lose your family if you continue to obsess' even if there's no chance of winning the object of the obsession. Reason has no part to play in it at all.

The Roman poet Ovid wrote a whole book on the subject of remedies for love (diets of various herbs, going hunting, dwelling on all the failings of the person who has so obsessed you), but he acknowledges that only two of them really work. The first is time. Once the object of the infatuation is removed, a total cure is obtained between a year and eighteen months later. The second remedy is to have sex with the beloved, and to actually win him or her completely. The crush will then disappear within three to six weeks. (I would recommend, for faster results, moving into the house of the beloved.) If the object of the crush says, 'I am yours! Let's live together for ever!' the crush might be over within two days. Obsessive love turns to the dust it always was, and the object of yearning becomes Home.

food for thought

Q *Have you ever experienced obsessive love?*

Q *If your partner became infatuated with someone, and you acknowledged (though your partner didn't) that it was an illness, how would you cope with it?*

Q *Do you know anyone whose marriage split up on account of an infatuation? What happened?*

Q *When you see that someone is in the throes of a crush at work, are you more amused or irritated?*

Q *Do you think obsessive love should be taken more seriously by the medical profession?*

Q *What do you think the difference is, if any, between being 'in love' and 'having a crush'?*

' on running out into a summer storm, naked '

A year after we were married my husband and I went with a group of our friends to a large, romantic house in Burgundy. One day it was particularly hot and, worse, humid, and we hung around the house and grounds in desultory fashion, scarcely able to think, let alone speak to each other.

Then in the evening there was a storm. I've never seen rain like it, one glorious power shower letting rip from the heavens, thunder thundering like it was the end of the world, and lightning which was almost continuous. How we needed that storm! It was as if we had been in a sulk all day, and someone had suddenly slapped us and snogged us and said, 'Come with me!'

Well, my husband responded to the invitation. He seemed genuinely transported, and did what he had never done before or has ever done since. He took off his clothes, right there in front of us all, and ran out into the garden. None of us said a word, but we watched him from the window.

How did we watch him? Enviously? Did we want to join him? Did we think he was showing off? Why didn't we join him? (Because we didn't.)

For my part, I loved him and envied him for running out into the storm. The truth is, he carried it off because he is tall and slim and looks good naked. If any part of him had wobbled (and that's where at least part of my envy resides – some of me would have wobbled) I would have felt embarrassed on his behalf. It was an aesthetic act, to be performed aesthetically.

What is interesting about this episode, however, is that the point of view of the observers (us) is so very different from the point of view of my husband. He never thought for a moment, 'I am going to perform a work of art for my friends!' His was an act of utter spontaneity, abandon, etc., and he wouldn't have got away with it if it had been anything else. Yet he increased *our* self-consciousness by being *unself-conscious*. Do we join him? No, we don't look as good as he does. Am I enjoying what I'm looking at? Yes, it's very beautiful.

If we really had thrown ourselves – and our most imperfect bodies – into the night and the rain, it would need 100 per cent participation (everyone as spontaneous as each other) to work. Just one outsider, looking askance, looking shy, would have spoilt the drama.

Imagine if mid ecstatic rain dance a dour French farmer came to watch from next door. Would he have thought it 'beautiful'? No, he would have thought, 'quite mad', and within a few seconds we would have agreed with him.

food for thought

Q *Can you imagine yourself running in a storm naked?*

Q *Would you be more likely to get out there if you were alone, with your partner, or with other people?*

Q *We were sober at the time, but I wouldn't have joined in even if I was drunk and everyone else had taken off their clothes. If you had had a drink or two, would that have made a difference?*

Q *If your partner ran out into the rain naked, would you think he/she was ridiculous?*

Q *Do you see the act of running out into a storm naked as romantic or simply silly?*

❛ on plato ❜

I read my first dialogue of Plato when I was sixteen. Up until then, schoolwork had seemed a dry and dusty affair to be endured until I could be reunited with my girlfriends with whom I could discuss the real stuff of life: namely whom we fancied, whom we had snogged, and whether any boy had ever touched us 'down there'.

But Plato was to change all that. I had always been intrigued by the idea of philosophy, yet when I'd browsed the philosophy sections in second-hand bookshops the subject had seemed so *dry* – all about the nature of language and logic. But Plato talked about *real* subjects: love, justice, whether you should obey laws even if you thought they were bad ones, whether knowledge was possible, whether our soul survived death; and not only that but the *way* he wrote about them was so brilliant. He wrote philosophy through the medium of conversation, two or more people arguing out a point to arrive at something called truth. Of course there was a little artistry in Plato, he knew in advance who he wanted to win (Socrates). But nonetheless, I understood the moment I read Plato's dialogues the full potential of *any* conversation: that it could be a mutual seeking of some sort of *truth*. What was good about a particular film/play/gig that you'd been to together? What made it better than something else? What was bad about it? The important thing is that it should be possible to *persuade* your partner that you are right, or *be persuaded* that they are right. Simply sticking to your point of view with no debate is dull; simply trying to win is dull. The deepest pleasure of a good conversation is when you feel yourself skipping up Plato's ladder with a friend or partner towards something called truth, or goodness, or beauty. When you have had an honest argument, changed your minds, and come together again. When you are both strong enough to give ground to the other for the sake of something more than either of you.

Plato is most famous for his theory of Forms. In the early dialogues the theory seems faintly absurd; there is a Form of Table that transcends the world which is the most perfect, most tably table ever conceived, to which we all unconsciously refer when we talk about *this* table. Ditto with hair and even dirt: somewhere out there in the universe is the dirtiest dirt imaginable, of the dirtiest consistency and the dirtiest colour, to which we unconsciously refer when we ask, 'is that dirt on the carpet?' As a theory of language – where do words come from? – it's interesting, but quite specialist.

Far more accessible are his Forms of Beauty and Goodness. Either these exist transcendently or they don't. It's quite tempting to say they don't, because where are they? And more to the point, absolutes don't exist. Beauty is in the eye of the beholder and all that; concepts of goodness are culturally bound, e.g. paedophilia is great for the ancient Greeks but not for us.

But if everything is relative, human beings have real problems. Nothing is either beautiful or good, but believing it makes it so. Child sacrifice is a good and noble gesture if you live in ancient Carthage and your gods require it of you. Cannibalism is good when you eat your enemies and not your friends and there's a shortage of protein in your diet. Genocide is good to solve problems of over-population or, perhaps, to create a pure-blooded master race. Goodness depends on your perspective, nothing more, nothing less.

I believe in goodness, and I don't think that's because I've absorbed the values of our society and am obedient to them. My belief is not rational, it's intuitive. When I recognise goodness in another person, I am uplifted. I do not think, 'This person has made a correct analysis of the situation and has behaved appropriately, according to such and such a protocol.' My heart is absolutely engaged. When Plato asks the question, 'Where does such a feeling come from?' his answer is, 'We have known the Form of Goodness since before we were born, our souls are immortal and have already been acquainted with it. In this life, therefore, we respond to a specific example of goodness by *recognising* its likeness to the Form.' It's bizarre, but recognising something out there, that really exists and is important, is exactly what it feels like.

food for thought

Q *When you have an argument, is it more important for you to learn something or to win?*

Q *Do you think it's a reasonable human enterprise to look for truth in a poem, novel, or work of art?*

Q *Is truth for you just a correlation of statements and facts, i.e the truth of the sentence 'There is a cat on the mat' depending on there actually being a cat on the mat? Or is there something more profound about it?*

Q *How important is it that you see eye to eye with your partner on the subject of truth?*

Q *Do you believe that beauty is always in the eye of the beholder?*

Q *Are you tempted to read some Plato now?*

‘ on changing
your mind ’

When I was a child I made two observations:

(a) that children were always changing their mind about things, like who they wanted to play with;
(b) that grown-ups never changed their mind about anything. They were *unpersuadable*.

I was so alarmed that as a child I made a resolution to be a constant friend, regardless of whether my friends were constant towards me, and as an adult a resolution never to be fixed in my opinions on things, and ready to change my mind at a moment's notice. It's difficult sometimes, and involves a certain lack of commitment to any particular idea. Like, how should I decide which political party to support? On the bonus side, however, it has meant that every conversation is a pleasure, because I might be a changed person by the end of it.

My mother was a very opinionated woman who never changed her mind about anything. She believed

(a) that she was above the law;

(b) that God was an invention of the upper classes to protect their interests, which was why she went to church at Christmas and Easter;

(c) that all those who performed charitable works were doing so for precisely the same reason as she poured herself a gin and tonic at six o'clock every evening; namely that it felt good.

For ten years I used every argument I could devise to try to defeat her on any one of these fiercely held opinions, but failed miserably. In fact, now I come to think of it, she may even have defeated me. I remember the day in 1973 when she leant over the rope in the Tutankhamen exhibition and picked up a large golden goblet to sample the wine therein, which, declared the happy notice beside it, had been reconstituted from the desiccated dregs that were found in it when the tomb was first opened. The shame of it! Whose mother could have ever done *that*? 'Yuk,' she said, 'honestly, they shouldn't have bothered.' And now – what has happened in the intervening years? – I look back on that moment with something more akin to pride.

food for thought

Q *When was the last time you ever changed your mind about something?*

Q *Have you ever changed your mind about something you considered important?*

Q *Have you ever managed to change your partner's mind about something important?*

Q *Have you ever thought that your partner is too stuck in his/her ways?*

Q *How often do you change your mind about someone you know, for example thinking that they are more or less likeable than your first impression?*

Q *Do you consider open-mindedness a virtue? If so, why do so few people have it?*

' on torture '

Is torture always categorically wrong? According to the Declaration of Human Rights, yes, and is so wrong that the radical Muslim cleric, Abu Qatada, who has recently been released from a British prison where he'd been held on terrorism-related charges, can't be deported to Jordan in case he is submitted to torture.

I obviously don't know this Abu Qatada, and according to a family friend he is charming and generous to a T, but imagine that he's co-ordinated some master plan, whereby a bomb goes off on the hour every hour in a different British city. He's arrested, say, after two bombs and sixty deaths and he's being interrogated at Scotland Yard. When he's asked where the other bombs are, he mocks the police and says things like, 'The trouble with you in the West is that you're all so weak, you deserve to die!'

The tenet I love most in the Christian religion is 'Love your enemy'. When it's observed, feuds cease, peace reigns, civilisation flourishes. Yet in such a situation as this would it really be right to stand by and watch another three hundred people die rather than lay a finger on him? Would the British people feel a sense of pride that our principles mattered more to us than the death of innocent people? The truth is, I'm not sure that they would.

Torture has always been a means to an end: conversion to a religion or the getting of information. If you found yourself on the rack during the Inquisition, consciously feeling your limbs wrenched from their sockets, you were more than likely to die. I've been told that in Saddam's Iraq there was one torture chamber for every thousand people, where electrocution of the genitals was a trusty favourite. In these cases the torture is evil, the end is evil: total submission.

But what if the torture is less bad, in that it does not permanently maim, and the end is good? What if, for example, a gang of child abductors in the US have been caught but will not tell the authorities where they have hidden the children? Should we allow those authorities to use their notorious 'waterboarding' technique to get information on the children's whereabouts? Apparently the information given under torture is unreliable, but isn't it worth a shot? Would you think differently if *your* child was among those abducted? Wouldn't you want to throttle them yourself until your child was back at your side?

Yet how clever the Americans would have been if they had run Guantanamo Bay with humanity and intelligence rather than the crowbar approach of 'We have ways of making you talk'. They might have brought in Muslim clerics who could have given lectures on 'The Political Agenda of Osama bin Laden' and 'Islam as the Religion of Compassion'. They could have said, 'We arrested you because we fear you and want to understand you. We fear for the future of the world. Teach us to live in peace.' Aggression begets aggression; understanding, understanding.

food for thought

Q *Whom would you most like to torture, and why? What methods would you choose?*

Q *If the Jordanians admitted they were going to torture Abu Qatada as soon as Britain deported him, do you think it would be wrong to send him off to them?*

Q *What is the greatest torture ever inflicted upon you?*

Q *Do you think torture can ever be justified?*

Q *Do you think Amnesty International is right to give America such a hard time on their use of 'torture' – i.e. sleep deprivation and waterboarding – when so many other countries in the world inflict torture which maims permanently?*

‘ on parties ’

My mother believed that pleasure was the only reason any of us bothered to get up in the morning, and that there was nothing that could beat a good party. And all the other mothers in the neighbourhood, which was a prosperous one, believed the same. This meant, in practice, that between the ages of fourteen and eighteen I went to a party almost every night of the holidays. I came to dread them. By the end I was begging my mother to let me have a night off; she wouldn't let me, she said it would be rude. I had to stay up, she said, until midnight, when my father would pick me up. From about 9 p.m. I began having visions of white sheets between which I could slip and sleep for ever. I didn't drink, and I didn't like pop music, and I didn't dance, so you can see what fun I was. What I liked doing, then just as much as now, was having conversations on such subjects as, 'Does life have a meaning?' But parties aren't quite the place for them. I used to feel an acute sense of loneliness at a party. So when I left home to go to university, I went, reluctantly, to about one a year, and now I'm thoroughly grown up I go to even fewer than that. Even if fifty Hollywood studs pleaded with me to dance the night away with them, I would choose a night in with a good French movie any day.

However, this would be my ideal party: a re-creation of my old school dormitory, where eight of us would sleep in two rows of four. There might be a few candles, a fire in the grate, and some sublime music. We would then lie in the dark and would know that everything we said was felt and safe and true. There. Completely perfect.

food for thought

Q *Are parties more enjoyable when you see old friends or when you meet new people?*

Q *Is your partner relaxed when you dance with someone else?*

Q *Are you able to let yourself go at parties? Do you need to drink before you can totally relax?*

Q *Do you enjoy the buzz of a party?*

Q *Do you often feel an outsider and want to go home?*

Q *Would you like to be invited to my ideal party?*

Q *Do you enjoy formal dinner parties?*

Q *Would you secretly prefer to be in bed at nine o'clock with a good book?*

❦ on humiliation ❧

When I was a girl my grandmother said something very wise to me. She said, 'If you can risk being humiliated, the world is yours.' She also said, 'When you're old like me, you will never regret what you did, only what you didn't do.' I took her at her word.

My favourite book and film when I was a teenager was *Far from the Madding Crowd* in which Bathsheba Everdene sends the stolid Farmer Boldwood a valentine card and writes 'Marry Me' inside it. I thought that was so cool, but couldn't think of anyone I wanted to marry, only kiss. So in bed at night I used to practise. 'Kiss me!' I rehearsed in the darkness. It sounded wonderful. I couldn't wait for the real thing.

Forget parties, parties were boring. Lifts, libraries, trains, planes, boats: I would spot someone I rather liked the look of and contrive an irresistibly romantic situation with them. It had to be a public place, I certainly didn't want an affair, and ideally I would never set eyes on the object of my embrace again. You see how like Bathsheba Everdene I was? All I *really* wanted to do was pronounce those magic words, 'Kiss me', and then see what happened next.

Sometimes, however, it all goes disastrously wrong. I was once on a yacht doing a night watch at three in the morning during a force 9 gale. I've never know anything so exhilarating: vast waves breaking within inches of me, any of them capable of dragging me into the sea. I shouted out to my companion – and he wasn't even my type, really, just in the right place at the right time – 'Kiss me!' but he just looked at me as if I had gone stark raving mad, and held on tight to the helm. Ah, those burning cheeks I suffered whenever I dared replay the moment! And the worst thing about this kind of humiliation is that friends are totally unsympathetic. They say, 'You said what? In a storm? Are you crazy?'

On the plus side, however, the man I'm married to now was once sitting opposite me in a library and if I hadn't dared . . .

Q *What is the most embarrassing thing that has ever happened to you?*

Q *Are you over it yet?*

Q *How badly does it bother you if you play a really bad game of football, or make a fool of yourself at a party?*

Q *Have you ever taken out your sense of humiliation on other people?*

Q *Have you ever been humiliated at work?*

Q *Have you ever humiliated someone in public, for example your partner?*

6 on education 9

A friend of mine taught French in a local adult education college for twenty-five years. She ran a breakfast club, and brought along croissants and French coffee for a 7.30 start. Her students would then proceed to chat in French for an hour, and occasionally she would butt in to help with grammar and vocabulary – just enough to make everyone feel that a little progress was being made, and a lot of pleasure was being had.

Then the Local Education Authority got to hear about the class. They were scandalised. Was the students' progress being recorded and graded? What exam were they working towards? When my friend explained that they weren't working towards an exam, the LEA described her classes as 'pointless' and closed them down.

Even now I feel a kind of incandescent rage when I think of this story. It typifies everything that is wrong with education today. Education has been reduced to grids and grades and league tables. In fact, if you can't measure it, then it doesn't count. Everything has to do with separating the sheep from the goats. And how do you tell a sheep from a goat? Examine them, of course!

Then send the sheep to university and tell the goats to get lost.

To carry on the metaphor a little further, it seems that every government forever, left and right, has made it their mission that all goats should become sheep. Goats get a little unruly; sheep know how to belong to a flock: they behave! Our education system today is like one large sheep pen. No, worse: even the sheep are further categorised into good sheep and bad sheep, some with a marketable value, and others with little.

How has it come to this? And what is to be done about it?

As a social phenomenon, I think it's quite straightforward. We said goodbye to the aristocracy (quite right too) and replaced it with a meritocracy. You were allowed to be a ruler if you were good enough to be so. How could you tell? Public exams! In the good old days, public schools existed for the formation of *character* – hence the cold baths, beatings and bullying. An academic education was seen, at best, as irrelevant for the needs of a young gentleman.

But then the grammar schools came along, and began to produce some very clever rivals. The aristocrat, who had once been particularly sniffy about cleverness (my father's mother was an aristocrat and particularly snobby about learning – 'hide yours at all times' she would advise me), was not to be outdone. Public schools now had to employ the very best teachers they could find, and they had the money to do so. It was as though the aristocrat had said, 'Golly, we have to be clever now to keep our place in the pecking order, do we?' and duly started to bring their schools into line.

For some time grammar schools outstripped private schools in academic excellence. A meritocracy really seemed to be on the cards. Social mobility was actually possible. But then people were upset about the eleven plus: it wasn't right that children should be written off before they were sixteen, surely? The establishment saw their chance: divide and rule. And the independent sector flourished once again: a return to the elite of old.

And now, what is to be done about it?

Possibly, we could close down independent schools. But independent schools are very good. And the reason is, they don't separate the sheep from the goats as is done in our state schools. They are not interested in a form of social control. Their selling point is they want 'the whole child' – do you want to act? We'll make you a star! To sing? Ditto! Play for England in your favourite sport? Look no further, you'll be representing England in the Olympic Games! Do you enjoy learning? We'll give you the best teachers! And the learning (unlike state schools) is orientated not towards exams but its intrinsic pleasure. One of my sons (aged fifteen) recently showed me a five thousand word essay he'd written called 'My Utopia'. He had to think about what a perfect society would look like. He won't get a GCSE for it; but what he will get for it is the beginnings of a mind at work, something far more valuable to carry him through his whole life.

In fact, if I were the Minister for Education I would confront the real evil: why is it that every school isn't like an independent school? Why is it that in this day and age the eleven plus has been replaced by a far more invidious entry qualification, money?

I groan when I hear that exams are going to get harder and the peripatetic music teachers are going to be 'let go'. Years ago I used to be a truant officer. Why did children truant? *Because school was boring.* Why do state schools have to be SO BORING? If I had power I would make schools irresistible. I would let children think for themselves, instead of indoctrinating them. I would let them make up dances, songs, write plays. I would teach them ethics from the age of five, encourage them to talk about God and the constituents of a good life. I would get them to keep diaries, I would encourage reflection, introspection. I would make them stand up in front of the class to talk about their families, what's good about them, what's bad about them. I would get them to read books, paint pictures, learn to draw, bake biscuits. I would encourage everyone to play sport in the afternoon, or, if they didn't like sport, I would take them for walks and teach them the names of the birds and the trees. And school would be the best part of the day, and every morning every single pupil would be eager to get back there.

People say that what you get lots of from a private school is 'confidence' or 'social capital'. Why can't every child acquire that confidence, regardless of parental income? Well, I have completed the circle. Because the state loves children who love exams. And the rest who don't, who gives a damn?

food for thought

Q *Our schools look after children for at least eleven years of their lives. What subjects would you teach them to give them a better start in life than they have now?*

Q *If grammar schools came back* without *an entrance exam, complete with Latin and Greek and harder science and maths, and opened their doors to anyone who thought they'd enjoy having a go, do you think they'd prove popular?*

Q *In Germany they have a two-tier education system – (a) strictly academic colleges, and (b) 'technical' colleges which teach their students how to set up small businesses and make money. The technical students end up richer than their more academic peers. If those who didn't go to a grammar school ended up with a better standard of living than those who did, do you think we would feel more relaxed about re-introducing grammar schools?*

Q *Would you say the point of school was to learn about life in the fullest possible sense, or to get good academic qualifications?*

Q *Do you think you made the most of your own education? Would you take up the opportunity of returning to college as an adult?*

Q *If you were Minister for Education and it was your brief to draw up a curriculum for the twenty-first century, what would you have our children learn?*

' on free will '

If free will really does exist, it's a miracle. A miracle is defined in my dictionary as 'an event or act which breaks a law of nature'. So to act freely is to act unbound by nature: you are the 'first cause' in a chain of events rather than a mere passive part of that chain. Modern rational men and women like the idea of free will (otherwise how could we ever justify punishing anyone?) but hate the idea of miracles. Surely there is a huge inconsistency here.

When I was a student probation officer I had to do a report on a thirteen-year-old boy called Joseph who was about to be released from a youth custody centre. There were two thick files devoted to his case: a single mother who found him impossible, a father whom he had never met. He'd been stealing since the age of seven.

It is extremely difficult, if not impossible, to distinguish nature from nurture. I was brought up to love parties, yet nowadays even the party scenes in a film make me squirm in my seat. Am I still rebelling against my mother? Am I carrying an 'anti-party' gene? Nature/nurture: it's bound to be some subtle amalgam in me of the two; and ditto with the boy Joseph: his appalling behaviour might never have been allowed to become habitual if he'd had a father at home, if his mother had been sterner with him (or gentler, perhaps), or he might just have been born the way he presented to me that particular morning: surly, defiant, dishonest.

I sighed. He was a handsome boy, and he looked me straight in the eye. Now, what was I going to say to him? Has your most recent spell in youth custody reformed you? Has it taught you a lesson? Are you going to stop breaking into people's houses now? I didn't bother to ask him. The answer would have been no on all counts.

So I lay back in my chair and sighed again.

'You don't know what to do with me, do you?' he grinned.

'Oh yes, I'm afraid we do. The science is indisputable. Do you know what I mean by DNA? Your genes? Your biology, what you're made of, what you can do nothing about? The truth is, my dear Joseph, that you were born a thief, and there is nothing I, or anyone else, can do about that. You have what's known as a genetic malformation. I mean, we are right in our diagnosis, aren't we? When you go into a shop or a friend's house, have you ever managed once to leave empty-handed? You are suffering from what we call the thieves' twitch, not dissimilar to the twitch in an old man's eye. Don't you find it completely impossible not to steal?'

He blanched and said nothing.

'Listen, I don't wish to alarm you. Some people commit crimes because they are naughty, mischievous, bored. But in your case, you are genetically malformed. We think we have proof. But don't worry, we treat these cases of genetic malformation very leniently, because it's not your fault you're a criminal, so how can we possibly blame you? And in fact I've come here today to tell you about the best, most comfortable prisons we have, because you're going to have first choice as to where to go. Do you like sport, Joseph?'

Joseph said nothing.

'Because some of our prisons have superb sports facilities nowadays. And there are others with really good libraries, where you can even take a degree or several at the Open University. It might be that as a younger man you opt for sport, and when you're in, say, your forties or fifties you go for the better education. What do you say to that?'

Poor Joseph, he couldn't speak.

'Or it might be that you'd like to be a cook? Is good food important to you? There are some prisons with excellent kitchens. And not only could they train you, but if you do well you could even work in a prison kitchen!'

Joseph was by now in a state of shock. I leant over and patted his knee.

'Please don't look like that,' I said. 'Life on the outside isn't much fun, you know. I mean, look at your poor mother, do you think it's fun for her? Real life is tough. Relationships, marriage, children, being continually disappointed at work – if you can find a job in the first place. You can have a really rewarding life in a prison and, hopefully, you'll see what I mean one day.'

About a month later, I heard from his mother that Joseph was a reformed character. She couldn't believe the change in him. He'd even bought her some flowers. I never found out whether Joseph's 'true' character ever came back; but if it never did, did his 'true' self only begin to emerge on that day? Nature, nurture, or something more exciting? Could it just have been an act of will?

food for thought

Q *Do you feel uneasy about my interview technique? I lied, but, temporarily at least, the interview had the desired effect. Do the means justify the end?*

Q *This technique is a well-known one. It's called the 'paradoxical injunction', and is used to make people re-examine their behaviour by asking them to do things which are unexpected, e.g. choose your prison – or can you wait till Friday to make a further suicide attempt? Would you use it on your own children?*

Q *Do you believe free will is a miracle? If your answer is no, why not?*

Q *Are you a thoroughgoing determinist, i.e. do you believe that even when we think we're behaving freely we are actually behaving entirely as our nature/nurture prescribes?*

Q *Can you think of an act of free will which has changed your life?*

' on bullying '

Bullying is nasty. In the same way as I might have a taste for chocolate, the bully seeks out weakness in others and feeds off it with relish. The trouble is, bullies often think of themselves as strong and cool. They can be of any age. If you're very unlucky, your boss might be a bully, or even worse, your partner. What is to be done with them?

I was bullied at school when I was about ten, in the traditional sense of being subjected to mild forms of torture. Some of it wasn't too bad: I was regularly pushed down into a foxes' den with a boy called Greaves and we were made to kiss while each and every boy (I was the only girl in the school) took it in turns to point a torch at us and enjoy the show. I rather liked Greaves. But I didn't enjoy the dead animals which used to greet me as I opened up my desk in the morning, and I particularly didn't enjoy being held down by several boys while some creep put live earthworms into a syringe and squashed them on to my face and hair. I've had a bad relationship with earthworms ever since, and gardening is especially alarming.

But my wise grandmother came to the rescue. She was bedridden and had long, white, silky hair and wore long, white, silky nightdresses. When any of our family – aunts, uncles, cousins, all of us – were in any sort of difficulty, we would ask to visit and open our hearts to her. I sat next to her on the bed and told her all. Her advice was pure genius.

She told me to imagine that I was an alien from another planet who'd come down to earth to do a research project. It was going very badly. Rumour had it that on earth there was a species of animal called 'human being', and human beings were known to be very cruel to each other. I had been briefed to find out exactly what this cruelty consisted of, but so far I hadn't spotted a single case of it. I'd been to coffee mornings, bring and buy sales, hospitals and churches, and was on the point of going back to my planet disappointed, mission unaccomplished. But suddenly, exclaimed my grandmother, you've ended up at Fan Court School! You can't believe your luck! There's as much nastiness as you could hope for!

After insisting that I had struck gold, she told me I had to get down to serious research. I had to write down exactly what they did in a proper notebook and call it 'Research Project on the Nature of Nasty Behaviour among Human Beings'. I had to observe their expressions exactly, and describe them as carefully as I could. And above all, advised my grandmother, 'Be like a scientist! Don't use words like "horrible", use words like "interesting".'

Within three days everyone was in awe of me. I wasn't cowed any more, I was cooler than they were. I just observed them as a biologist might his specimens, the power was all mine. My grandmother did that for me, just like that.

food for thought

Q *Were you ever bullied at school?*

Q *If you met your bullies now, would you remind them of how they treated you?*

Q *Did you ever bully anyone?*

Q *Would you rather hear from the teacher that your child 'picks on' the younger children or is 'picked on' by the older children?*

Q *What would you do to stop bullying at school or at work? Would you stick up for an employee you felt had been unfairly treated?*

Q *Have you ever bullied or been bullied by your partner?*

Q *Why do you think people bully?*

‘ on the difference between power and freedom ’

Once upon a time a fisherman was dozing by his boat on a beach in the midday sun when he was rudely awoken by a passerby.

'What time do you call this?' said the man. 'It's the middle of the day. You should be working.'

'I've done my work for the day,' said the fisherman. 'Now, if you'll please excuse me, I'm resting.'

'You'll never get on in life resting, you know,' said the man. 'You should be building another boat, and then hiring other fishermen. Then your haul would be many times as large.'

'Why would I want that?' said the fisherman.

'To get rich, of course. Then you'd be able to buy a large house and wear fine clothes.'

'Why would I want that?' said the fisherman.

'One day you'd be rich enough to employ others to do all the work for you. You'll have all the free time in the world, you'll be able to rest all day, if that's what you want.'

'What do you think I'm doing now?' asked the fisherman.

In my mind, the fisherman won the argument. Hands down.

But the story highlights the difference between power and freedom very well. People sometimes confuse the two. Isn't power being able to do what you want, exactly when you want? Nothing could be further from the truth. Being at the helm of government or some multinational corporation makes you responsible for thousands and even millions of lives. Henry V bemoaned *'What infinite heart's ease must kings neglect, that private men enjoy!'* He loathes the *'throne he sits on'* and *'the tide of pomp'* and, above all, *'thrice-gorgeous ceremony'*, and envies *'the wretched slave, who with a body fill'd and vacant mind/ gets him to rest'*. Nor is it just potentates who suffer so: celebrities might be able to click a finger and get the object, woman or man they desire at that particular moment, but where is their freedom? Even if they bought themselves an island and an army to fend off the paparazzi, even if they took their loved one to a romantic spot on that island which no one would ever discover, the chances are that when the loved one's ditched and feels unadulterated rage, lurid scenes of exactly what went on in aforesaid romantic spot will be splayed over the pages of every tabloid. The celebrity is no freer than a dog in a gold-encrusted kennel. Why, for God's sake, is that what 70 per cent of our schoolchildren want to be?

But the life of a man who is perfectly free is not much better. The man with no attachments, no responsibilities, no dependants to work his guts out for, not even a wife to bicker with, lives in a sort of void. No one could call a tramp a happy man; in fact, he stands as a warning to others to be wary of freedom. There has to be a life between these two extremes that suits us. But in the end, what matters more to us, power or freedom?

food for thought

Q *Does your job have too much or too little responsibility, or is it just about right?*

Q *If you have children, does responsibility for them make you anxious?*

Q *Have you ever been tempted to walk out on your life because you can't take the responsibility?*

Q *Have you ever responded to a beautiful road or path by yearning to travel down it?*

Q *Do you veer more towards a love of freedom or a love of power?*

Q *If you feel differently from your partner about the relative merits of power and freedom, do you respect his or her perspective?*

ʻ on being irritated ʼ

Being irritated is often harder to deal with than being angry. When you're angry, you have a row, you make up. When you're irritated, the crime is often so minor it's not worth mentioning. So you keep quiet, endure, and the irritation gets even worse. What is to be done?

I was twenty-two when I married my first husband. There was a lot about me which irritated him. He would snap, ʻDon't say "notepaper", say "writing paper"!ʼ I dutifully obeyed, and meekly agreed that he was right about everything.

However, when we separated I saw that he might have been a tad dominating, and resolved that if I ever found things irritating about a future partner I would rise above it and shut up.

I tried. God, how I tried! I was being tied up in knots. There were two things about my second husband which irritated me hugely, both totally trivial. In all ways, he was noble, kind, intelligent. But he cut the bread in steps, never going quite to the bottom in a clean slice. And worse, he said the word, ʻpleasantʼ. At first I would say to myself, ʻRelax, you are married to a wonderful man, and if he chooses to say the word "pleasant", then who am I to judge him? He could do far, far worse!' But every time he said it, my soul would seize up, and I would think, 'No, no, nothing is pleasant in this world! Things are either terrible or wonderful or mediocre. Never, NEVER "pleasant"!'

In the end, I knew I had to be dominating. I said, 'There is something I have to confess.' I think I must have looked anxious. He was so relieved when I told him what was bothering me that he never said that excruciating word again; though his habits of the breadboard live on to this day. He was also able to tell me that he didn't like the sound of a spoon thudding against the palate of my mouth when I ate yoghurt, and I now only eat yoghurt like a princess, or in private. What do other couples do about each other's irritating habits? Are people open about what annoys them about the other? Or do they suffer in silence?

food for thought

Q *Is there anything that really irritates you about a partner, sibling or friend?*

Q *Do you generally speak up when something he/she does irritates you?*

Q *If your partner or friend asked you not to use a particular word, would you obey?*

Q *Have you ever done anything practical, such as buying your own private tube of toothpaste to manhandle as you choose, to avoid being irritated by your partner squeezing only from the bottom?*

Q *Which of you is the more tolerant?*

❛ on jewellery ❜

When my first husband asked me to marry him, he gave me a ring of ludicrous splendour. I was a penniless undergraduate at the time, eking out an allowance of £20 a week, yet on my finger sat this emerald befitting a pope. The ring was an heirloom. It had been bought in India in the mid nineteenth century, and numerous great and splendid women before me had not only worn it but had their portraits painted wearing it, and those portraits to this day hang in a vast stately home. I wore the ring the whole time: during lectures, supervisions, doing the washing-up. I wore it with jeans and a T-shirt. To me it was the most romantic ring in the world.

Then one day my mother persuaded me to take it to Bonhams to have it valued. She told me she was having valuations of some of her own jewellery for insurance purposes; why not just enjoy the look on their faces when they see it? I went reluctantly. I didn't want to think it had any value, except to me. We would never be able to afford the insurance anyway. I'd feel obliged to have it locked in a bank somewhere.

The stone was a fake. There were twenty-two diamonds surrounding it, so the ring had *some* value, but nothing like what we had anticipated. My relief was enormous, and my pleasure in the ring completely restored. Some ancestor had obviously fallen upon hard times, and had sold the original stone. Good for him. And good for all the ladies who wore it thinking it was the genuine article, when in fact it had no more value than a little piece of green glass washed up on a beach.

Q *If you knew a piece of jewellery was worth £100,000, would it make it more or less pleasurable to wear?*

Q *If you knew that your fiancé had spent less than £100 on your engagement ring despite being well off, would you feel irritated? Hurt? What if the ring was incredibly beautiful, but was made of, say, polished basalt or granite? What if it was just costume jewellery, sparkly and charming but with no monetary value?*

Q *There is, I think, a very real connection between money and love. In high-profile celebrity divorces, where couples fight over millions, the need for money seems barely distinguishable from the need for love, or at least for affirmation. Likewise, when parents die and children squabble over who should inherit what, it's as though they're all six years old again fighting for their parents' love. Have you any direct experience of love and money being confused?*

Q *If you inherited an heirloom, which you were morally obliged never to sell but to leave to the next generation, would you give a damn about how much it was actually worth?*

Q *If you were told about a favourite piece of jewellery of yours that the stones were fake and it was worth nothing, how upset would you be?*

Q *Your grandmother, whom you were close to, has left you a diamond bracelet which you quite like, but which you would never actually wear because it's out of fashion. You keep it in your jewellery box along with your favourite pieces of costume jewellery. The box is stolen. Would you be most upset about the loss of your grandmother's bracelet? If so, would it be because of what it was worth – you were thinking of selling it anyway – or because of its sentimental value?*

❛ on identity ❜

When I was nine years old, we moved into a very large house and I had a bedroom on the top floor. If I shouted, no one could hear me. Every night, my mother used to turn off my light at ten to eight, before she and my father had supper together, and she would get incredibly angry if I turned it on again. I wasn't remotely tired, and would lie in bed for hours just thinking.

There was a burglar I used to think about, so often and so vividly he may as well have existed. He used to climb up the drainpipe outside my window. I would watch the curtains move and know that within a few moments he would be with me in the room. Sometimes, when he appeared, I would tell him to take what he wanted but to leave me alone. Otherwise I would threaten him with the lion who slept under my bed. Eventually I became interested in who this burglar was. He was obviously light and agile, because when I looked in the morning the drainpipe was as fixed to the outside wall as it had ever been. This must mean, I reasoned, that he was young – no more than twelve or thirteen. And one day, when my mother and I went to the cinema together in Staines, I even saw where he lived.

I noticed an old, dirty block of flats with washing out to dry on a balcony and I knew instinctively that that was where I could find him in the daytime, if ever I could be so bold.

As I grew older, our conversations became more interesting. For example, was it entirely wrong that he, who was poor, should be robbing me, who was rich? What defence did I have? I knew in my bones it was still wrong, but I had no arguments, and often he would outwit me.

Then I wondered: if my parents had adopted him at birth, if he'd gone to Harrow with my brother, would he still be a burglar? Of course not. And even more intriguing than this, if I had been adopted by his family at birth, would I be a burglar? I just didn't know.

So who was I? My first husband accused me of believing the self to be like a red, shiny billiard ball rather than something dynamic and moving, like a stream. And yes, it's true – that I have an essential self has always been my instinct. But when I think, I talk to myself in my head, and the voice that I used to think of as 'mine' turns out to be more about social class and history than about 'me'. If I had been adopted at birth, even the voice sounding in my own head would have been different. Where is this person, then, that I can call 'me'? What can I finally call my 'essential self'?

I have always rebelled against everything: when my mother made me go to parties I rebelled by teaching myself Greek; when she sent Valium to my little sister at her boarding school, insisting it was 'quite a wonder drug and she should try it', I rebelled by teaching Greek to my little sister. When she insisted that we should have as much sex as possible while our bodies were still young and trim, let me tell you, I almost signed myself up at the local nunnery. So, is it a biological gene which commands me to do the opposite of what I am asked to do? If so, what sort of pathetic identity is that? Is my soul no more than a binary response mechanism, which turns itself off when others are on, and on when others are off? I like to imagine that I have integrity when perhaps all I am is one large reaction to the circumstances about me.

Anyway, the years passed, during which time and to my absolute delight my bedroom really was burgled while I was away at boarding school, and the jewellery I'd inherited from my relations, and for which I cared not a jot, stolen. (I remember sitting on my dressing-table stool, looking in the mirror, musing romantically: 'Who was this stranger who came to my room? Would I have liked him? Would he have liked me?') And one day, a few years later, it dawned on me that I wanted to work with these strangers. I wanted to make them my friends. And even more importantly, I wanted to meet my alter egos. As far as I was concerned, every burglar was a version of myself.

And that's what came to be. One evening a week I would teach young offenders social skills. I was all alone in a Portakabin with eight of them. No one was supervising me, thank God, or perhaps Health and Safety would have closed me down. We sat round a table, like a dinner party, and I said to them, 'I want to talk to you about identity. Now, you all think of yourselves as burglars and cool thugs about town, and I think of myself as posh. But can't you see the randomness of that? Can't you see that it might just as well have been the other way round, that you might have gone to posh schools and worked in banks, while I might have been cleaning out offices after dark? Because there's no essential difference between us. It's just a difference in our manners. You're here to learn social skills, and let me tell you, no one knows about social skills better than the upper classes. It just happens to be what they do best.'

When I was in training, the building opposite our School of Social Work was a Teacher Training College. Sometimes I used to cross the road and have a cup of coffee with the trainee teachers and ask them what they were learning. One of the subjects was 'psycholinguistics', which, in a nutshell, requires that you 'respect the language of your pupils and do not undermine their confidence by correcting it, either in speech or writing'. What I did next was a knee-jerk reaction to the stupidity of such a philosophy. If you write well, and speak well, you get a good job. Blow your working-class identity! Is it right that teachers should just correct the grammar of the middle classes?

So, in my irritation with a system that had so failed them, the first thing I did was to teach my young burglars how to speak proper: to sit tall and enunciate their vowels. I then taught them the mannerisms of the upper classes, and how to walk like a gentleman, how to look someone in the eye and nod politely. I taught them how to air-kiss on each cheek, and the exact noise which accompanies the air-kiss. On one perfect evening I had them lining up to kiss me, one after another, and I gave their performances marks out of ten. And when they spoke and moved as I wanted them to, with an easy nonchalance, I made them all members of the Cabinet. We sat round the table and discussed the social problems of Britain, and what to do about them. They were the most charming, witty, intelligent company I have ever known. As far as I know, none of them ever reoffended, or not while I knew them, and I might even have been quite pleased with myself if it hadn't been for a chance meeting with my favourite, a handsome boy called Charlie Fletcher (a notorious Cambridge burglar who'd even burgled us), who told me with great pride that he was dating a girl from a very fancy boarding school. 'Oh God,' I thought, 'what *have* I done?'

food for thought

Q *Do you think you have an essential self?*

Q *Do you think having an identity means identifying oneself with a particular group, i.e. gay, black, feminist, Old Etonian?*

Q *Do you think it's important for your mental health that you should have an identity?*

Q *Do you feel an outsider?*

Q *Do you enjoy a sense of belonging, to a group, a club, or even to your extended family?*

Q *Do you feel you belong to a particular social class?*

Q *Would you like to see an end to the class system, or do you think that wherever there are people, social classes will always exist?*

‘ on ghosts ’

In my university application, the only word I wrote in the section entitled 'interests' was 'ghosts'. I saw a ghost when I was twelve. My grandmother had taught me how to arrest a dream if I didn't like it. Before you go to sleep you say to yourself 'Pinch your ears, pinch your ears' again and again, and if you're frightened in a dream that's exactly what you do, you pinch your ears. When you don't feel anything, you know you've outwitted your sleeping self and you half wake up. Your prize is a 'lucid' dream, and as a child I really knew how to indulge in these. I could fly at will. I could become part of a proper story, instead of being at the mercy of whatever dreams flung at me. And the moment you are bored or scared, you can decide to wake up completely and be shot of it.

When I saw the ghost – it was a horrible thing and this book is no place to relive that night – I pinched my ears hard and the ghost just stood watching me, jeering. I hid under the bedclothes for twenty minutes, slapping myself, pinching myself, waking myself up, telling myself it was an hallucination. But when I dared to look again the ghost was still there. I spent the whole night trembling, and as soon as it was morning ran into my parents' bedroom. Their attitude was, so what if it was a ghost? These things happen. Just don't tell your brother or sister because you'll frighten them.

All four of my grandparents and both of my parents have seen ghosts. My mother and grandmother saw one at the same time. They were staying in the attic of the Wheat-sheaf hotel in Virginia Water (which is still there), because the other rooms were full. A kind ghost came to sit on the bed of each of them in turn; a woman, full of tenderness. Neither was frightened in the least. In the morning they learnt that many other guests had had the same experience, and one of them had actually bothered to research who the mystery woman was. Apparently she had been employed in the house as a nanny, and both of her young charges had died of polio within days of each other. My grandmother and mother had been staying in the children's bedroom, and the heartbroken nanny had never deserted them.

My husband is a sceptic, like all those who have never seen a ghost; except in his case, he has. One twilight on a Northumberland beach he noticed a fisherman wearing an old-fashioned fisherman's smock, mending a creel. He was rather charmed by the timelessness of the scene, but, when he walked past, the figure suddenly disappeared, as though he'd been imagining the whole incident. Again, he was not the first to see the fisherman: he even had a name, and had died in a storm a hundred years previously. Now he says, 'I might just have been dreaming. The place was so evocative.'

But the best ghost story, because it's not one that has

been told and told again (and embellished every time), was one related to my husband on an aeroplane. He was chatting to the woman in the seat next to him, a university professor, and because my husband was still shaken by his own eerie experience on the beach, he asked her whether she had ever seen a ghost. The woman was tentative at first, but then agreed to tell him of her own experience.

'No one knows this,' she said, 'except my husband and my aunt, and it's only because I see you're sympathetic that I'm telling you. I've kept it quiet all my life for fear that people might think I'm mad. But this is what happened.

'I'd just had a baby and we'd decided to call him Edward after my uncle who had recently died. I hadn't had any drugs during the labour and felt completely well. Suddenly my uncle was there right beside me, totally solid, there was nothing ghostly about him, and he said, "I'm so pleased you've decided to name your son after me!" and he talked about other things too, that only he and I would have known about. And then he left.

'The following day I went to see my aunt and told her what happened. I said, "But there's one incongruous thing. He was wearing a suit that he would never have worn in real life. It was loud and yellow and American, with large checks. Completely unlike Uncle Edward."

'My aunt said, "Take a look in the wardrobe. Was that the suit he had on? He bought it a week before he died."'

Ever since hearing her story I've had a new respect for fashion. Make sure you like what you wear: you might be wearing it for an eternity.

food for thought

Q *Do you believe in ghosts?*

Q *Do the above stories irritate you because they were obviously made up, or do they bring to mind other ghost stories you've heard?*

Q *Why do people enjoy reading ghost stories or watching horror films?*

Q *Psychics say there is a difference between a ghost, which has no consciousness and is something like an 'imprint' of a previous life, and a spirit, which has a more active presence. Do you think they might have a point?*

Q *Do you have*

   (a) NO interest in the supernatural, believing it to be a load of bunkum;

   (b) a SLIGHT interest, but remain sceptical;

   (c) more than a slight interest. The possibility of there being another realm of existence excites you.

Q *When you die, would you prefer to have no consciousness whatsoever or to be able to watch over your children and grandchildren?*

‘ on suffering ’

When I was a girl of six I came across a small phial of poison in my father's desk. I asked him what it was for. He explained that he'd been issued with it when he was a pilot in the Korean War. There might be an emergency, in which case death would be a kind thing. I told him I didn't understand: why would anyone ever kill themselves on purpose? Sometimes, he said, suffering can be worse than death. I can't remember the examples he gave me, but I immediately realised he was right.

Two weeks after this epiphany I lost my shoes. I was a dreamer, I used to take them off in random places at the bottom of the garden, and my mother would shout at me and tell me how useless I was. On this occasion she told me to put on my walking shoes or we'd be late for the dentist, but I couldn't find those either. I was too terrified to confess. Death was the only option. I went over to my father's desk to retrieve the poison, I was quite ready to die, and in death, I reasoned, my mother would forgive me. Unfortunately the poison was gone, and I had to face the music.

The legacy of this little tale is that I have never understood why more people didn't just kill themselves. When the news showed images of starving Biafran children and casualties of the Vietnam War, I wanted to write to someone and say, 'Don't you see! These people would be better off dead! Can't we send them some phials of my father's poison?'

As for me, my threshold for suffering is zilch. I had a happy, uncomplicated childhood and the only major upset in my life was when my first husband left me. From that, I learnt about loss: not just my own, but that of any 'displaced' person or refugee; also the feelings of those who'd lost a job they'd loved, or experienced the death of someone close to them. I tell my second husband that if he dies before me I'm going to build a pyre in our garden and jump up next to him mid-conflagration. I was strong once: nowadays I feel I would be useless at facing any tragedy, I shall just want to slip away from it. Yet who knows? Perhaps some nobler instinct will kick in, for those who still need me.

We see a lot of footage of war in our family – one of the consequences of having five sons. So much of it is painful to watch, but the sight which really appals me is the marching. I study the soldiers' faces, blank and cold. I watch their feet and their boots, on and on through the relentless mud and snow. I think of their frost bite, their blood-soaked socks, their memories. These men don't know when they will either rest or eat. They don't know when they will die. What hope, what instinct drives them on?

All I know is that no instinct would drive me on. I would ask to be shot, I think, soon after my first blister gave me trouble, or I was cold for more than a few hours.

A last thought: there is a famous theological debate about why a beneficent and omnipotent God should allow suffering. Yet I've never understood why it has warranted so many books and so much attention. Imagine a world where there is no suffering. Where would there be room for goodness, courage, compassion? Even love itself would become trivialised. Without suffering, there would be no meaning to anything, no truth; or the bland truth of a barbecue and FUN FUN FUN. Give me a pyre in the back garden any day.

food for thought

Q *The Hindu practice of suttee – derived from the Sanskrit word meaning, 'faithful wife' or 'virtuous woman', and being her action on her husband's death, namely throwing herself onto her husband's funeral pyre – was outlawed by the British Raj which thought such a custom barbaric. But given that we are better able to express our emotions nowadays, especially those of unadulterated grief, and given the fact that we are culturally and religiously eclectic, is now the time to bring back the time-honoured practice of suttee? Or, allowing that the reintroduction of funeral pyres would not be environmentally friendly, at least some eco-friendly alternative, such as a pill-popping wake?*

Q *How much suffering can you bear? What kinds of suffering, mental or physical, would be impossible for you?*

Q *Would you enjoy life more or less if it was one big party?*

Q *When you see a friend suffering, how much do you suffer with him/her? Or do you count your blessings?*

Q *Would you say that you and your partner have suffered an equal share of 'the slings and arrows of outrageous fortune', or that one of you has had the lion's share?*

Q *Has there ever been a certain rivalry in your partnership over who has suffered, or who suffers, the most?*

' on sex '

Why is sex so fascinating to us? Perhaps you saw the subject in the contents' list and jumped to this conversation first. My son, an internet journalist, tells me that if the story he writes has a sexual element the chances are it will get 100 times more hits than if he simply sticks to politics, which is such a depressing fact that my instinct now is to bore you all into submission. Though even submission has its zealots.

There is nothing deep or mysterious about sex. Aristotle said that having sex is less interesting than creating something or thinking a good thought, because animals can't think or create. The pleasure human beings have in eating and sex simply reminds us that we're part of the animal kingdom after all.

There is a great children's story about stone soup. A beggar persuades a rich king that nothing beats a good old-fashioned stone soup. So he's allowed into the kitchens to make some. He puts his stone into a large cauldron of water and tastes it. 'Mmm,' he says, 'it's good, but it needs a little seasoning. And then it needs an onion and a carrot. Perhaps a parsnip or two. And celery really sets off the taste of a good stone.' When the king tastes the soup he finds it quite delicious. The beggar is suitably rewarded and a cookery book commissioned.

Sex is like the stone: depending on the ingredients you add to it, it can be either good or bad. Spicy, hot, unfamiliar, exotic – sex with a new partner can be amazing. But affection, humour, familiarity, ease: these are also happy bedfellows of sex. If you have a long-term partner, this is what you have to play with.

The million-dollar question is, 'Can sex be spiritual?' We are always hearing of the wonders of 'tantric' sex, and I've even read the *Kama Sutra*, but still I have to be persuaded that it can be. When I see 'spiritual' sex in a film I turn away in embarrassment. I think, 'Sex is *so* weird.' It's the films like *Last Tango in Paris* which are actually sexy. And a quick survey of my friends suggests that while it is more meaningful to have sex with someone you love, sex itself seems to have a life of its own. Which is, of course, why we're so gripped by the subject. If it was the normal, loving thing that human beings do to each other in a long-term relationship, would we really be so obsessed by it? We love sex because, however hard we try to persuade ourselves it isn't, sex is *naughty*. It's the one place we don't have to behave ourselves. It's sport without the rules.

But if sex is akin to a sport, what if one of you likes playing tennis, so to speak, and the other doesn't? Before I got married for the first time – I imagine at a totally inappropriate moment like packing for my honeymoon – my mother warned me *never* to tell my husband that I had a headache or was too tired to have sex. 'Sex is like a good walk,' she told me. 'You might not feel like it at first, but you'll soon be in the swing, and then you'll be pleased you took the exercise.'

Do I agree with her? For once, I probably do. Saying yes is friendly; say no too often and sex becomes a thorny issue.

What really annoys me is when therapists see something 'deep' about the reason why one is off sex or not reaching orgasm. They assume it's to do with the relationship, that the relationship is hitting the wall. Rubbish: it's to do with the stressful job or the children who sap all that sexual energy. There are couples who loathe each other and find their hatred a real aphrodisiac; there are others who love each other and haven't had sex for years. They should all be left in peace.

food for thought

Q *If sex is important to you, why is it?*

Q *Do you talk about sex with your friends?*

Q *If you knew that your partner was playing out a major fantasy with a film star while having sex with you, would it bother you?*

Q *Have you ever worried that something your partner wanted to do was kinky?*

Q *Do you think that love and sex go hand in hand, or at least ought to?*

Q *If you knew you were never going to have sex again, how much would it bother you? Would you rather lose your eyesight?*

Q *How much do you think about sex when you are away from your partner?*

‘ on environmentalism ’

Environmentalists are passionate people, and recently I heard of one who'd sued his employers for unfair dismissal. Apparently, he'd been over-evangelical on the subject and the bosses didn't like it. He'd wanted his beliefs to be accorded the same respect as a religion.

Did he have a point? Is environmentalism the next religion? Well, it certainly shows signs of becoming one. To begin with, modern culture is steeped in environmentalism. We are taught about all the major religions from about the age of five, thus preventing the 'internalisation' of any of them; and we learn that belonging to a religion is more like being part of one great big happy family than the acceptance of some revealed truth. Yet the focus that has drawn schoolchildren together is the protection of the environment. When my own children were young, they knew more about 'Captain Planet', the hero who brought pollution down to zero, than they did about Jesus Christ. As yet, however, there are no decent traditions – even meeting your mates down at the bottle bank has been replaced by door to door collections by the council. And certainly no rituals. But there could be, if some charismatic leader told us all to go to the forest and sing.

Surprisingly, the metaphysical component of environmentalism is rather high. In the Old Testament, we are seen as guardians of the earth, and the Psalms are full of gratitude to God for the radiance of the natural world.

Recently I was arrested by the beauty of a frozen puddle in the road. The cracks in the ice were perfectly symmetrical; the sun was shining on it. No kaleidoscope in the world could have been more beautiful, nor have told me so much about the mystery of physics. I stood there, jaw hanging open, for ten minutes. I ended up being late and irritating a friend who didn't, on this occasion, have much time for me and my puddle. But wasn't I feeling something like awe before the divine? I love the fact that there's no evolutionary advantage to being struck by such a silly thing. Do lovers of beauty (when they should be concentrating on their tasks) make better mates or parents? Love of beauty in nature, which I suppose is the number one reason why anyone should be an environmentalist, is as metaphysical as you can get.

On the downside, however, a religious war is a distinct possibility. A crusade against non-environmentalists, who would, after all, be letting the side down by spending money on all the latest power-hungry gadgets and forgetting to recycle the packaging. Perhaps shooting down fly-tippers would be no bad thing. But what if James Lovelock is right, what if our problems stem from over-population, what if the earth can sustain one billion people but not the seven billion we have now? Lovelock believed that 'Gaia' – Greek for 'Earth' – behaves like one large organism that ultimately has its own interests at heart. Gaia doesn't want to be polluted and destroyed by mankind. So it's in the process of shaking us off, with a little global warming and a few pandemics here and there. The fanatic environmentalist would, of course, be working for Gaia. How can six billion people be destroyed in the most environmentally friendly way? His ways will certainly be subtle. Beware.

There are huge moral dilemmas facing those who wish to save the planet, even if the less apocalyptic scientists, who believe we really can affect the future of the world, turn out to be correct. For example, how are we to tell one billion Chinese people that they oughtn't to have washing machines? Do we remind them of their heritage, that their ancestors made their living in laundries for hundreds of years? Do we sponsor a Chinese family who want to apply for a washing-machine licence by giving up our own? (That would be a truly holy thing to do.)

When I was at school we were posed the following dilemma: do we suffer three hours of painful dentistry *now* or an amputation when we're seventy-five? We all chose the amputation. How much do we really care about our children's children's children? Would we see our own standard of living drop substantially to make sure that our successors will be able to enjoy the same country walks that we enjoy?

I am, I'm sure, an environmentalist of a sort. Can anyone not be? Let's say a big yes to pollution in our rivers! It wouldn't make sense. And if there are two scenarios, the first in which the self-destructiveness of humans has resulted in their extinction, but the earth happily survives us and sees a return to the Garden of Eden, or a second, in which the earth has become parched and arid, and seven billion people – or perhaps eight billion by then – are waiting patiently to be transported to other planets in their super-duper time-travelling rockets, I know which I would choose.

food for thought

Q *Does thinking about the future of the planet depress you?*

Q *Would you like to do more than you already do to 'reduce your carbon footprint'?*

Q *Even though you don't like the idea of pollution, are you too worried about other things, like work or children, to give much time to thinking about it?*

Q *If the polar ice caps melted, resulting in the flooding of two-thirds of the earth's surface and killing two-thirds of the earth's population, how much would you care, as long as the Western world remained unscathed?*

Q *Could you see any advantages in a mass cull of humankind, if you knew their deaths would be quick and painless?*

Q *If you had to choose between the survival of the earth as we know it and the survival of mankind, which would it be?*

' on god '

When I was a child lying in bed in the dark, I realised that the only important question in life was whether God really did exist. My mother said no, my school said yes. I decided that my mission in this life would be to find out the answer. To that end I wanted to be locked at the top of Rapunzel's tower with an unlimited supply of books, and when I was near my death I would write the answer down on a piece of paper and throw it to the winds. No one in my imagination caught the piece of paper, but it would have been a life well spent.

What struck me then as they do now are the consequences of there being a God, or no God. On the one hand, life is pregnant with meaning. Every action, good or bad, is a significant one, with a particular relationship to Truth. Or, conversely, life is ultimately as meaningless as a game of Monopoly. Of course, you can invest huge emotion in throwing the dice, buying property and getting rich, and suffer terribly at the whims of Chance – and these emotions are real and powerful: hope, dread, longing, victory! – but at the final reckoning, so damned what.

The atheists' bus, which declared on its side, 'There's probably no God. Now stop worrying and enjoy your life', not only acknowledges life's intrinsic meaninglessness but says, so what, enjoy! But it can be very difficult to stay in the game, blinkers on, especially if you're losing. Even if you're winning, sometimes you might pause to wonder, like Truman Burbank in that wonderful film *The Truman Show*, what would happen if I break through the boundaries of the Game? In fact, what's a midlife crisis but some feeble, half-thought-out attempt to do just that?

People often say, 'I don't believe in God, but I am a good person.' But they are not so much good as 'good', according to the rules of the Game. It is 'good' to help in the community. Move forward three spaces. You have been witnessed doing a 'good' act. Spend an evening at the Mayor's party. You gave up smoking on the advice of the Government. Well done! Use the money saved to buy yourself a new pair of shoes. If you argue, 'No, no! I'm not *good* just because I'm obedient, I'm good because I *like* goodness!' Watch it: that smacks of metaphysics to me, something *more* than man, rather than something we've just made up as we go along. May God be with you!

food for thought

Q *It seems astonishing to me that someone can write a book called* The God Delusion *without once discussing God: not one line! Richard Dawkins wrote about religion, which is an altogether different subject. Religion is about man, not God. It's made up by men. It's about what we do when we seek the transcendent. Often what the religious do, particularly to non believers, seems strange and bizarre. But surely the quest is the right one, and those who never even begin the journey are more spiritually lazy than intellectually acute. Would you consider yourself spiritually lazy? Or, looking back on your life, do you think you've made a reasonable attempt to understand what something 'totally other' might be like?*

Q *If you knew absolutely that there was no God, would it make you feel differently about your life? Would you feel liberated or enchained?*

Q *If your faith in God is steadfast, has it been with you since childhood, has it grown over the years, or is it the consequence of an 'epiphany' – a life-changing event?*

Q *Do you envy or despise people who have an unquestioning faith in God – or are you one of them?*

Q *If two of you go to church and both consider yourselves Christians, would you let the other know if you were having severe doubts about your faith? Or would you wait until you felt more committed again before discussing your anxieties?*

Q *'God is not about this or that doctrine; God is about Truth and Goodness.' Do you have some sympathy with that statement, or do you feel that Truth without doctrine is something flaccid which doesn't hold up?*

Q *What does 'Truth' mean to you?*

Q *The philosopher Wittgenstein famously said, at the end of his* Tractatus, *'What we cannot speak about we must pass over in silence', and with that one line he inspired shelves of theology books. The great mystics all argue that there is a particular holiness in silence. Do you think there's too much talking in religious worship?*

❛ on human rights ❜

Where do human rights come from? The sad thing to me is the fact that something as noble and good in intention as the Universal Declaration of Human Rights, written in the aftermath of the Second World War, should have been reduced over the last decade to a humanist philosophy that has lost its way and become the butt of jokes. Human rights come from the same stable as religion, but don't admit it. To a large extent they are culturally bound – Muslims are correct to accuse the original Declaration as being Judaeo-Christian biased and not 'Universal' at all, in that 'rights' seem to mysteriously belong to individuals rather than communities. But religion unashamedly searches for some transcendent truth, true for all people and for all ages: its bedfellow is metaphysics, we all know that (and often distrust it for that very reason). What is intensely irritating about the creators of modern human rights is that they declare their own charter as gospel. They pretend to despise metaphysics, and yet that's exactly what they're doing: creating gods.

In the Game of Life, rights are rules which get made up halfway through the game when states have amassed enough money to buy (a) star players who can tell us what the new rules are, and (b) the apparatus by which these new rules can be enforced.

When the Game of Life was first played all those thousands of years ago, before money was invented, naked human beings had no rights at all. In fact, they had fewer rights than the modern dog or cat. No right to healthcare, because there were no doctors, no right to an education, because there were no schools, no right to work, no right *not* to work, no right, even, to live or die; or do you believe – and beware, you might just be stumbling into metaphysics again – there is something intrinsic about simply *being human* which accords us mystical protection?

Today I read in the papers – wow, what fun it must be to be a star player in Strasbourg! – that human beings have a new right. The Court ruled that the presence of a crucifix in the classroom could 'disturb' children of other faiths or none, and that it 'violated pupils' human rights'.

If anyone reading this happens to be a judge in Strasbourg or knows someone who is, please remember me when you've got a job vacancy. Pick me! Pick me! If it is one's human right not to be 'disturbed', think how many rights we have to put in place – your work is barely begun, O judges! We could Cancel All Noise for a start, because lots of people find noise disturbing. And horror films. And grisly stories in the newspapers. We could cancel marital disharmony, visits to dentists, and all questions with no answers. In fact, let's make a clean breast of it: anything that upsets the equilibrium of a pleasant life should be outlawed immediately.

My Pilates teacher received a directive instructing her

not to use the word 'anticlockwise' as in, 'Swing your arms in an anticlockwise direction.' The word 'anti', explained the missive, had 'negative connotations' and she was advised to use the word 'counterclockwise' from now on. I confess – alas, what a reactionary I must have been only a fortnight ago – that when I first heard about the directive it seemed absurd. I couldn't believe that someone, some-where, was being *paid* by an organisation to tell us that the prefix *anti* didn't contribute to world happiness. But now I am a convert. Surely we human beings need a right to protect us from ever hearing anything negative ever again. Let's make the world one great, big, wonderful, happy YES! We can do it! YES WE CAN!

food for thought

Q *Do you believe that there are fundamental human rights? If so, can you justify them?*

Q *Have you ever felt that one of your basic human rights has been infringed? If so, how and when?*

Q *If you were a judge at Strasbourg, what rights would you invent?*

Q *Do you ever feel nostalgic about the times when actions were simply thought to be right or wrong?*

Q *If you are not what is called a 'positive' person, would the removal of negative words from everyday language help you to see things in a different light?*

‘ on body parts, dead or alive ’

One question which has always intrigued me is how much attachment people feel to the various parts of their body. Do people feel that their arms, for example, *are* them, or do they feel that they belong to them, in the same way as an item of clothes or a house does?

One of my aunts has a fine, aquiline nose. When she was younger all her female cousins would tell her, ‘You *must* have a nose job!’ But she resisted, saying, ‘My nose is me. This is who I am.’ And my own mother, who was far more distressed than I was at the size of my bust at fourteen, promised me that after my children were born she would pay for the best breast reduction surgery in Harley Street. When the time came and I resisted, she accused me of having a ‘sentimental attachment’ to ‘what was not beautiful’ and would become ‘pendulous and bothersome’ when I got old.

The funny thing is, we do not choose our body parts from some kind of antenatal catalogue yet we instinctively feel they are very much *us*. Is that because we have grown into our bodies? Or do our bodies take their cue from our personalities and grow into us? It's a paradox that our culture, nominally so holistic, recommends shopping for different body parts if we can afford it. Or the problem can become even more philosophically complex: 'Inside every fat woman, there's a thin one! Inside every ugly woman, there's a beautiful one!' So that I, who *seem* ugly on the outside, am *really* beautiful, and I *need* surgery because I am a holist and believe that the external qualities of a person should reflect his or her internal qualities. Gosh. You see quite how complicated it can be.

A few years ago everyone got very upset about the body parts of dead babies being stored in jars of formaldehyde without their parents' consent. These babies had often died *in utero* and were being kept for research purposes. Alder Hey, the hospital in Liverpool where these infant bodies were so irreverently treated, is now synonymous with just how wicked and uncaring doctors can be, snatching young babies away without so much as a by your leave, then labelling them and putting them in jars. In those days doctors treated dead bodies as simply that, dead bodies, never imagining for a moment that their little misshapen forms could have spiritual significance for those who had lost them. Nowadays, we say, we know better. Those bodies were *human beings* and needed to be treated as such. So their dead remains, fifty years on in some cases, were adopted, grieved over, dressed in pretty white and yellow frocks and had 'blankets of love' knitted for them before being given a full and proper Christian burial. It seems interesting to me that as we lose God we have to turn the body itself into something mystical.

A final thought: if you own your body parts, should you

be entitled to sell them? Should it be possible to sell your kidney, for example, for £100,000, or however much you can get for it in the marketplace? We don't like the idea of it at all. Our own bodies, we feel, should be priceless. But we're happier about donating our organs: I would be incredibly happy to give a kidney to one of my children, for example, or indeed to my husband. Even to my sister. But what if I happened not to like my sister? What if she's undermined me all my life, had an affair with my husband, and is now at death's door after a car accident? Do I give her my kidney? Conversely, would I expect her – just because she's family – to sacrifice her own kidney for me? No wonder family Christmases are tricky. It might not be kidneys we give each other, but sometimes it sure as hell feels like it.

food for thought

Q *Do you think of yourself as someone who happens to have the body you have, or is your body integral to your identity?*

Q *Can you imagine giving one of your kidneys to a friend if you knew it would save his or her life?*

Q *If your friend was rich and gave you a cheque for £100,000 as a thank-you for 'your sacrifice', could you be persuaded to cash the cheque? How much might you accept?*

Q *Have you ever considered cosmetic surgery? Might you consider it in the future?*

Q *If your eighteen-year-old daughter told you she was spending all the babysitting money she had saved over the years on surgery to increase the size of her bust, how hard would you try to dissuade her?*

Q *Do you think the practice of saying goodbye to a dead body, perhaps even kissing the hands or cheeks, might have any therapeutic effect?*

❛ on flirting ❜

I take flirting extremely seriously, as did my mother, grandmother and both my husbands. By 'flirting' I do not mean trivial coquettishness, a fluttering of eyelashes, a pouting of lips; or, as exemplified in the male of our species, an embarrassing reeling off of compliments and *double entendres*. No! Flirting is an art form, a highly intelligent, sensitive, driven way of getting to know someone in as short a time as possible. It is about breaking their guard, the ultimate prize being total possession.

When I was thirteen my mother took me aside and told me that the time had come to instruct me in the art of flirting. I felt flattered and was keen to learn. This is what she taught me:

(a) Assess your prey. Is he cocky or shy? Is he handsome and knows it, handsome and doesn't, or not handsome but with your help could become so? If he's God's gift to women, ignore him! Look over his shoulder as though looking out for someone else. When he addresses you, be rude. On the other hand, if he is self-effacing and shy, leap on to his knee.

(b) Get to know him. You are a failed flirt if you utter one word about yourself. Ask anything. Be open, direct. Ask him questions that no one will have asked him before.

(c) Flatter him. If he is handsome, tell him he is intelligent. If intelligent, handsome.

(d) Remain mysterious, and don't tell him much about yourself. Flash your eyes as if you have hidden depths. But then stand back, don't let him enter. At most, give him a tempting morsel, nothing more.

(e) You will only achieve total possession if you back off at the very last moment. Play it cool. Make him think you want him, and then run away. Possession is now achieved.

(f) These rules will apply for your whole life. Never imagine you can take a short cut: not even in late middle age.

My dear mother then told me I should practise on our hair-dresser, Franz. I did so. Franz did very well in acting out the kind of shy, gauche boy I might meet at a party, and after-wards I looked back at my approving mother and asked her, 'Am I really to jump on to his knee?' I think she let me off the hook on that occasion; but I was certainly still jumping on knees at eighteen, and my first husband, a vastly intelligent studious type in glasses, thought it heaven.

food for thought

Q *Do you flirt?*

Q *Does your partner think you flirt? If so, does she or he mind?*

Q *Was my mother's advice sensible or immoral?*

Q *Would you like to have been trained in the art of flirting?*

Q *Before you first went out together, was one of you the flirt and the other the flirtee, so to speak?*

Q *Can you remember how you won each other? Would you feel embarrassed to repeat your wooing strategies with each other today? If not, try them.*

Q *Do you think the art of flirting should be taken more seriously?*

' on charity '

This conversation might as well have been entitled *On Guilt*. This is where I fall short on my obligations to the rest of the world in a big way. But what are those obligations? What is charity?

When charity is thought of as 'love' I'm good at that. My favourite part of a church service is called 'The Peace' when you embrace your neighbour on the pew, which, it's true, is a bit more social than godly if you already know them, but if you don't you feel a wonderful sense of kinship with all humanity. You feel, 'We're all in this strange world together, mate, and we'll make the best of it, you and I.'

I know this about myself: that if I'd lived a hundred years ago I would have done all that I could for my community; and more, I would have wanted to change things. I would have been passionately political. Nowadays it is very difficult to be passionately political, because poverty in England isn't about money any more, it's about culture. And we, the middle classes, feel so anxious about imposing our culture on others that we don't bother.

The difficulty about charity is that there is a power relation between the person who gives and the person who receives. The one who gives has the power; the one who receives just has to grin and say thank you. No wonder the 'needy' hate being given people's cast-offs, while the middle classes happily scour the racks in charity shops for bargains. No wonder Africa hates being given our out-of-date medicines, when we at home don't even bother to look. Does this mean, then, that if we give we have to remain anonymous so that the person who receives doesn't have to feel grateful to us? If charity, on the other hand, is love, doesn't that make helping someone else part of a personal relationship, not a power relationship? Yet most people I know would feel hugely insulted if I wrote them out a cheque: their pride would always be greater than their need.

So basically what we do is to give through charities, so that we feel good and no one has to feel indebted to us. Yet even this is very, very difficult. My bank account usually hovers around zero, but sometimes I get a windfall and it is one of the sweetest pleasures I know to imagine how I might spend it. The feeling is light, expectant. I find myself looking in the windows of shops, feeling I've won a raffle prize and that anything might be mine. The sum I'm talking about is £150 – never enough to invest or treat too seriously, but enough for a beautiful pair of new boots. And then the autobank tells me to donate my money to Africa, and I freeze.

A couple of years ago our Bishop came to visit the village church and he told us 'Christians' in no uncertain terms that it was our duty to give one tenth of our income to the Church, or to Church-sponsored charities. I collared him afterwards and asked, 'What if I'm in debt? Is it my duty to get more in debt?' He told me that I should 're-prioritise'. I had to think about that. I am conscious of the need to support our local shops and we even have a real live milkman: but should we be opting to shop in Asda and pass on any savings we make to charity? We have one holiday a year and go out to dinner on our wedding anniversary – should we be forgoing those? We have a lovely house and garden, bought long before the housing boom: should we be selling up? Our cars are worth £300 each: not much leverage there.

So when I get the letters from all these charities asking for money, my head seizes up with anxiety. I keep them, I don't even throw them away. I always think, 'One day, I'm just going to be so, so generous.'

food for thought

Q *Do you think you give enough to charity? Is £2.00 per month to NSPCC enough?*

Q *Do you feel anxious in the same way as I do?*

Q *Is the fact that you don't have any surplus cash a good reason not to give to charity, or do you think you can always scrape up something, no matter how stretched you are?*

Q *Can you imagine setting up a charity?*

Q *Would you prefer to help a charity with your time and volunteering rather than write out a cheque?*

Q *Does it make you feel good when you've been generous to those less fortunate than you are?*

Q *Do you make a point of giving to local charities, medical charities, or developing countries?*

Q *Who is being the most moral:*

(a) *the person who puts money away for his future so that he will never be a burden to others;*

(b) *the person who actively supports local pubs and shops, and raises money for the community, by helping with the church fete, for example;*

(c) *the person who gives her money to the most needy people, in developing countries?*

' on parenthood '

They say that those years when you are a parent of young children go by in a flash: enjoy them. I beg to differ. I have been a parent for twenty-eight years and it's felt like a lifetime. And 'enjoyable' isn't a word I would use when I remember being in the absolute thick of it. In fact, when I travel by train I avoid the carriages with the squawling infants, and I am utterly unsympathetic to the whining and relentless demands of the young of our species. I was not born a mother, I was made one.

When I was pregnant for the first time there was no book on parenthood that I didn't read at least a dozen times. I also bought myself a book called *A Colour Atlas of Life before Birth* and I would spend hours poring over the photographs of unborn babies until the day I realised that one of them was being held in a pathologist's clamp: a less charming title might have been *Pictures of Dead Babies*.

I gave up being a 'good mother' very early on. I made one nutritious meal for my oldest son (smoked haddock in milk, mashed potato and peas) and after watching him toss it across the room I'm afraid it was Milupa for ever, for the whole brood of five. I have broken every rule in the book.

The survival and happiness of my children have been infinitely less important to me than my own, so here, for what it's worth, is my philosophy of child-rearing.

Children can all expect two things of me: constancy and kindness. And that's more or less it. If I threaten them with a punishment (which is, in our family, always the same – two packets of sweets on Saturdays instead of three) then I always remember to carry it out. But I've never nagged and I've never shouted at them. If they fail to do their homework, that's for them and their teacher to discuss. It takes too much effort to make them do anything. I want to preserve my energy for *me*.

Forget the naughty step. Forget sending them to their room. I'm the one who runs away from *them*. I make myself a cup of camomile tea, take a good book and just go to bed, whatever time of day it is; I apologise, I say, 'I'm so sorry, I just don't like the way you're doing this or that, or the way you're whining and whingeing, I'm so sorry, I'm off to read a book.'

Then, bedtimes. For years I tried to do these properly: the bath, the tea, the story. But then I just gave up: I was too tired and too bored, and ended up falling asleep on the bed next to them.

So twelve years ago, when my children were aged thirteen, eleven, ten, two and a baby, I decreed that my own bedtime was nine o'clock and anyone wishing to go to bed before that time I would tuck up in bed with a story and anyone wishing to go to bed after that time would tuck me in bed with a story. My older children thought this was great, and in fact being asked how my day went and about the best thing that happened to me and the worst thing that happened to me (which was what I used to ask them when I was a 'good mother') was somehow really moving and restorative. I would always tell them the truth.

I think I can honestly say that I have never been remotely ambitious for my children, nor possessive, nor controlling of them. Perhaps that's simply because I have so many. Or because when I used to go to mother and toddler groups those competitive mothers appalled me, and even drove me on one occasion to show off, which reduced me to such self-hatred that I swore that forever more my tongue would be tied.

Children are not reflections of ourselves. They are not 'mini-mes'. If they are driven to be hugely successful entrepreneurs, great. If they choose to live in a hole and read philosophy, I shall probably feel closer to them. If, when they are older, and I am older, they treat me as I hope I have treated them, with constancy and kindness, that is all I could possibly ask of them.

food for thought

Q *Why does anyone ever have children?*

Q *Have you ever regretted your decision to have children, since the future of our world is so uncertain?*

Q *Have you learnt anything about yourself by being a parent?*

Q *Do you wish you had more children?*

Q *Do you think having children has made you a better person?*

Q *How would you define a good parent?*

Q *Do you think I have been a bad parent?*

❛ on forgiveness ❜

A long time ago I had a friend who volunteered to take my dog for a walk when I went up to London for the day. She forgot. When I got back home my pathetic Labrador was half-crazed, and there was shit everywhere. I rang her; she laughed. 'I'm such an airhead,' she said, 'I'm so sorry.' I didn't accept her apology. I didn't make a song and dance about her failure to keep a promise, I am far too grown up for that. I just dislodged her from that place in my soul called 'trust' – or rather, she dislodged herself, and I did nothing. She had not properly understood the distress she caused both my dog and myself; her apology was merely verbal, and consequently without value. I haven't forgiven her to this day.

The human acts of apology and forgiveness are among the most subtle, intricate and wondrous acts that human beings do. To apologise is not just to understand that you have done something 'wrong' but to understand the hurt that that wrongdoing has caused. To forgive is even more demanding, because it requires a leap of faith: you do not know whether the person who is apologising is play-acting or is genuinely remorseful. If you are the kind of person who cannot feel remorse, who says 'sorry' because it's convenient and not as a description of an inner state, then no one, I'm afraid, will ever forgive you more than once. Remorse is not just a feeling related to an act in the past; it is also a commitment to change in the future. One love affair is often forgivable. Beware the person who has a second.

There are people who believe that forgiveness does not require an explicit apology. You do it on your own: you let go of your negative feelings towards someone. I have never mastered this and never intend to. Providing they don't make me bitter, a few negative feelings towards people who have hurt me in the past are strangely warming and life-affirming. When my friends express anger with people who have behaved badly towards them, I join in, passionately. I feel human, healthy, well. Insulting those who have insulted you is terrifically therapeutic.

There are people, however, who never forgive their parents for being bad parents. They even seek them out, accuse them of doing this and not doing that, and demand an apology. But parenting is not a profession: parents are human and a home is *their* home too. Unless your parent really did you a bad turn, and set out to do so, to forgive what is less than perfect seems the generous thing to do. No apology necessary.

food for thought

Q *Do you feel there is someone out there to whom you owe an apology? Is there anything you would like to apologise to your partner for?*

Q *Do you tend to feel more guilt about your neglect of other people – partner/friends/family – or yourself, for example you're unfit, lazy and prone to a few lies here and there?*

Q *How best might you be forgiven, or will you go on feeling guilt regardless?*

Q *How difficult would you find it to confess to something you've done wrong?*

Q *Do you think people in general feel too much or too little guilt?*

Q *Do you think you are better at apologising or better at forgiving, or are you bad at both?*

Q *Do you feel angry with someone at the moment whom you would like to forgive but cannot, because they refuse to acknowledge how they have hurt you?*

' on touch '

A long time ago, when my mother came to visit me in hospital shortly after I had given birth for the first time, she looked aghast at my son who was splayed, fast asleep, across my chest.

'Careful,' she said. 'He'll get dependent on you.'

When she left I burst into tears: hormonal, doubtless, but I also understood for the first time why I suffer from a syndrome known to my mother and her cronies as MTF, a shameful condition in which the sufferer Must Touch Flesh. I can hug for England. In fact, in the last twenty-four hours I've hugged the BT man for fixing my phone, the man in the toyshop, the fishmonger, and practically anyone who's come to my door. I fall into their arms and belong to the world again, I feel physically earthed. When I see and touch no one all day, even when I drape myself in soft blankets as a substitute, I feel empty. God save me from heaven if all we do all day is some sort of spiritual blowing of kisses. I want and need the warmth and realness of other bodies.

It appals me that those bogeymen, the human rights creators, argue that our right not to be touched trumps our right to be touched; that teachers in primary schools can no longer put their tearful young charges on their knee, that physical touching between employees is discouraged. This is based on the premise that touching is fundamentally all about sex.

Kant said that touch is when the mind becomes visible. When I touch, skin to skin, I underscore what I feel about the person: gratitude, affection, maternal love. Who was it who translated these into a sublimated sexual drive? Who was it who said that touch was the first step to full-blown sex? Even if some post-Freudian hard-line analyst decrees that this is the case, the dreadful thing is that our risk-averse culture suggests that even if the number of sick minds is small let's cancel all physical contact *just in case*. What sort of sad generation are we bringing up?

My mother warned me about paedophiles: 'There are some pathetic men out there who like touching little girls. Don't panic, just say "no", be polite.' I was touched once by a paedophile when I was about nine or ten, a trembling hand seeking out a naked thigh. I thought, 'This man is pathetic,' just as my mother advised. The episode remained in a bracket on the edge of my experience; I was never remotely fazed by it. It's just hysterical adults who think children ought to be. (I'm not talking here, of course, about serious sexual assaults.)

The real problem is not that touch will suddenly become sexual between parents and children, teachers and pupils, friends and colleagues. The real problem lies paradoxi-cally in the one arena where touch is still permitted: couples. This is where the borderline between affectionate touch and sexual touch is the foggiest, and where the one might just turn into the other. That's great, if it's what you both want; and it's dire, if one of you is simply too spent to deliver and the other feels rejected. You might even reason that it's better not to be hugged in the first place and avoid the scenario altogether, and before you know it there's a steel wedge between you, right there in the bed.

I don't know what the solution is. I only know that affectionate touch within a marriage is ten times as important as good sex. Sex is about hormones, desire, biology, adrenalin, pleasure. Affectionate touch is first and foremost about love, and the physical expression of that love. In fact, touch outdoes talking a hundred times over as a means of communicating. If conversations about difficult subjects are simply too exhausting after the demands of work and children, then over the kitchen table take up your partner's hands and kiss them.

To hug and to touch needs to be uncomplicated, and sometimes in a marriage that has to be learnt all over again. Touching is the recognition that there really is another human being out there. And if we all did substantially more of it, how much saner and happier we would be.

food for thought

Q *Were you hugged a lot as a child? Do you think your approach to hugging (whether needing a lot or a little) is something that you learnt as a child?*

Q *Do you find it easier to hug your children or your partner?*

Q *Is it difficult for you to hug your partner in bed without desiring them sexually?*

Q *Have you ever avoided hugging your partner (though you have wanted to) because you thought it might lead to sex?*

Q *If, as a matter of routine, you were to spend two minutes after supper either hugging or consciously touching the other, would this make you feel closer to your partner?*

Q *If touching was incorporated into our daily public life – as in hugging, holding, patting etc. – would this be a good thing? Or do you think touching is unprofessional?*

Q *Primary school teachers are trained not to touch their pupils, even though instinct might dictate otherwise (such as after a fall in the playground). Do you think, given the public obsession with paedophilia, that such strictures are necessary?*

⸲ on nagging ⸲

I come from a long line of terrifyingly powerful women on both sides of the family. They were wonderful in many ways: vigorous, life-affirming, dangerously honest. But in one way they upset me hugely as a child. They all nagged their husbands. They reduced them to men who were not men: 'Yes darling, I'll get round to it, I promise,' those poor men would say, drained from a week's work while their wives were frolicking on the golf course. When we were fifteen, my cousin and I made a pact. When we grew up, never would a single nag issue from our lips. We would plaster, paint, wallpaper and mow; carry heavy furniture, put up bookshelves – anything rather than demand one iota of help from our partners. I've just this second been speaking to my cousin's husband. We have kept true to our word.

Women are famously manipulative. Or perhaps, simply clever. I have, in the past, simply turned all the lights off in the house except one; and under that one has been an item that I have failed to fix, by which I've left a screwdriver.

'Oh,' says my husband, victoriously, 'I see you've been trying to fix the light fitting. It was the fuse, you know.'

I congratulate him and tell him he's a genius, and we're all as happy as can be.

All of us, except my sister. She tells me I have 'bred a dinosaur', 'a man who does not pull his weight around the house'. I argue that he empties the dishwasher every day, for which I am eternally grateful.

'But does he cook? Does he clean? Does he put the children to bed?'

I argue that if he did those things we would have to miss out on our evening game of Scrabble; we wouldn't listen to music or, indeed, have a conversation. And anyway, he earns vastly more money than I do, it's his privilege to chill out when he gets the chance. But my sister won't have any of it. It's the *principle* of the thing, she says. And as for me, I'm just a 1950s housewife.

Quite honestly, I don't give a damn. Should I?

food for thought

Q *Do you nag?*

Q *Do you feel nagged and resent it? Or do you secretly quite enjoy it, as your partner reminds you of your mother?*

Q *Does your partner have a particular voice which he/she uses to nag with? If your partner were to sing the request would it make a difference as to whether you carried out the task?*

Q *Were you nagged as a child? If so, has that made you nag more or less as a parent?*

Q *If you are the main nagger in the partnership, have you ever considered simply doing the stuff yourself, or would that be against your principles?*

Q *Are you more like my sister, who insists on justice and equality in her relationship, or like me, who'll do anything for an easy life?*

‘ on depression ’

Even the word 'depression' is depressing. 'Depression' makes me think of geography and heavy weather. It also makes me think of a deep, slow, mind-numbing sadness, a low, flat hum of an existence. Yet when I hear that after heart disease, depression is the most common 'illness' in the UK, I can't get a handle on it at all.

I used to work in a psychiatric hospital. I know what mental illness looks like: the rocking, the anguish, the hallucinations, the paranoia. I even know that if a psychiatrist is both clever and lucky enough to hit upon the right medication, very ill people can get better. I have seen diagrams of what might go on in the brain during a mental illness; I understand that different pills work on different parts of the brain, depending on the nature of the illness. I also understand that the brain is an organ like any other organ of the body, that it is made of physical stuff which simply might stop functioning well, in the same way as the kidneys or liver might stop functioning well. But for me there is a very real difference.

If I were a British doctor researching the two most prevalent diseases in Africa, for example, Aids and malaria, I would be looking through my microscope, I would be working in a laboratory. An African doctor, researching heart disease and depression, would find his work far more problematic. This is because the causes of a physical illness are, by and large, physical and the causes of mental illness are to a large extent (despite an unlucky genetic pre-disposition) reactive to a difficult episode or accumulation of episodes in a person's life. In other words, the causes of mental illness are *unquantifiable*, which is why the African doctor would have such trouble.

There are understandable reasons, however, why the medical profession are so keen to make depression 'clinical', and bring it under their own umbrella. Society has always been kinder to those who suffer a recognised physical illness rather than the more obscure mental one. By presenting mental illness in the same bracket as a bad case of 'flu, society might be persuaded to look more kindly upon it. Yet in their determination to do so, they have inadvertently turned ordinary human misery into a pathology.

A few years ago my uncle endured a wretched death: his last few weeks were spent in intensive care. He couldn't sleep. The lights in the unit were on all night, and one by one the various organs of his body failed. He told his wife and the doctors that he wanted to die, he just couldn't take any more. 'Oh' said the doctors, 'Now his brain is beginning to fail too. He's got "clinical depression". We'll have to treat that as well.' If the doctors had said, 'What's he's going through is a terrible experience, for anyone, so we're going to give him happy pills to make him feel better', I would have had no problem. But the implication that his unhappiness was on a par with the deterioration of his body upset us all hugely.

At the moment the medical establishment is keen to

medicalise bereavement, too. At the last count you were allowed to be seriously unhappy for two weeks after the death of a loved one, but after that you can be deemed to be suffering an 'illness'. There is that much pressure on us to be happy at all times.

At university we all used to suffer from what we called *existential angst*. What do we do about the problem of the *existence* we are saddled with through no fault of our own? *Angst* is a wonderful German word which is more interesting than our 'anxiety'. It implies there are too many choices and human beings get stuck like a rabbit in the headlights. Sometimes I feel this in a supermarket when I am lost in aisle 24 far from any natural daylight or means of orientation. I will myself to faint so a nice ambulance man will carry me on a stretcher and I shall wake up in a hospital with friendly faces all round. Am I the sufferer of a mild case of Munchausen's syndrome, or just human?

Funnily enough I think the reason why society has traditionally been so nervous about depression – and is therefore so keen to turn it into an illness like any other – is that it's played out at the interface between the self *and* society. The individual who suffers depression *can't fit in,* and he's simultaneously *pushed away.* Life becomes dull and lacklustre, the 'fun' other people seem to be having unattainable. When I talk to friends who are depressed, there seems to be a real feeling of *exclusion from what's going on in the world,* to the extent that they stop caring. Yet what is this thing called 'society' anyway? It's a body of people, i.e. everyone else, who make huge demands upon you to be like them, as successful, happy and sorted as they are. To the extent that they give you pills if you're not.

The life of a human being is difficult to negotiate: we are social, yet we require solitude. We yearn for self-fulfilment, but then discover that self-fulfilment is dependent on others: other people have to like our pots, paintings, designs, novels or self-fulfilment doesn't work. The West is an extraordinarily difficult place to live: in our liberal society, never has there been more puritanism; in our love of success, never has there been less opportunity to succeed; in our love of freedom, never have there been more demands on us to think about things *exactly so*; in our desire to create, never in our history have we been told we have to have a good degree first; even in our simple human desire to help others, we are first vetted and examined.

If I were an African doctor researching the causes of depression in the Western World, I would not be looking at diagrams of the brain. I would be looking at *us*.

food for thought

Q *If you yourself get depressed from time to time, is it more for a reason you can point to or existential angst?*

Q *Why do you think that depression is so much more prevalent in richer countries than poorer ones?*

Q *When you feel miserable, are you able to talk about it with a close friend?*

Q *What, for you, makes life worth living?*

Q *Would you be patient with a friend or partner who slipped into a depression? Would you be less patient if you couldn't see any obvious reason for it?*

‘ on snogging ’

I experienced my first snog two weeks before my fifteenth birthday. It was quite as disgusting as I knew it would be, and I knew it would be because I'd practised with my cousin Sarah and the mere touching of another person's tongue with my own was a close second to having live earthworms put down my shirt.

Sarah was trying to help me out, and prove to me that my fears were irrational. She'd been snogging for months and thought it great fun. On the night in question, the last night of the Easter holidays before going back to my single-sex boarding school, I told her, 'Tonight is the night.' But the question was, which boy was I going to kiss? They all looked equally dreary. Sarah said, 'I'll tell you what, coz. I'll kiss three of them and tell you who kisses the best.' She duly did and, incidentally, is just as kind and thoughtful to this day.

She recommended Jeremy Brown, because the other two were 'outrageous and slimy and would put you off for life'. Jeremy was a pert kisser, clean and harmless, his tongue more like a wet, prodding thumb than a rabid slug. I endured that first kiss with barely a grimace. Yet, that

I should ever have to repeat the experience filled me with horror.

But then I fell in love and, of course, where there is love, kissing is the most wonderful thing you can do. Only three months after that first debacle I pinned my poor physics teacher against a wall and told him to kiss me. In the meantime, I had kissed two of my male cousins, one on each side of the family, and was getting a taste for it. When I was older and boys asked me to go to the cinema, I had little interest in the film. And when I got married at the age of twenty-two, it somehow got written into our marriage contract that I was allowed ten snogs a year with other men, and that wouldn't count as infidelity. Sexually I was both inexperienced and rather pure. I was also obedient. I counted those kisses religiously, and never went beyond ten.

When I married a second time, at the age of thirty-two, my new husband was appalled at that arrangement. He argued that a snog was a sexual thing, while I argued it was an extension of ordinary kissing, with romantic undertones. Anyway, snogs outside marriage were banned.

The other day we were possessed by a burning curiosity to know which of our friends still went in for snogging; and, if they had given up, why and when they had. So I rang my girlfriends, and my husband spoke to his colleagues at work. The average age of our little survey was forty-eight.

The result was: 20 per cent still kiss romantically as they had as teenagers, not necessarily as a prelude to sex; 45 per cent gave up kissing a long time ago, about which fact several women but no men felt sad; 35 per cent kiss only as a prelude to sex.

It makes me feel incredibly sad to think that a day exists in the future when I shall kiss passionately for the last time. To me, that seems far worse than dying.

food for thought

Q *In our survey, more women than men enjoyed kissing. Has this been your experience?*

Q *Do you remember your first kiss? Have you told your partner about it? If not, might you now?*

Q *Have you had any really awful experiences of snogging?*

Q *If your partner confessed to having a snog but no more at the annual office party, how upset would you be?*

Q *If you saw two old people snogging, would you think it romantic or disgusting? Would it depend on whether they were (in your eyes) still sufficiently physically attractive?*

Q *Would you feel relaxed about exchanging a boiled sweet with your partner, mouth to mouth? Or do you think that would be too unhygienic?*

Q *Do you enjoy the first kiss in romantic films?*

Q *Which is the more exciting for you: the days leading up to a first kiss, or the days between a first kiss and actually going to bed with someone?*

‘ on the morality of shopping ,

How ought you to spend your money? Should there be an *ought* in that question at all? What is the exact relationship between morality – the attempt to do what is right – and going shopping? This is, for me, a particularly difficult question to answer.

I'm not talking here about eco-shopping and being an 'ethical consumer' and 'sourcing your products'. That is a can of worms in itself – do you support your local farmer or the fair-trade co-operative in Kenya? Think of those air miles! I'm talking about the shirt I bought in the January sale from the rack at the back of the shop over which a sign declared NOT IN SALE. It cost me £200. It was made of the finest undyed Italian linen and had restoration frills round the cuffs and neckline. It was expertly cut and made me look – which is difficult – not fat.

When I like something expensive in a shop I feel the blood rising in my cheeks, a sort of private blush. I have visions of the starving in Africa, the homeless in London. I have visions of the Barclaycard bill in a month's time. Then there's another voice: 'I like this shop! I know the owner, his wife and the girls who work for them. There's a recession on and I need to support small businesses. What's more, I need to support those who wove this cloth, and the designer, who is a complete genius. To buy it would be to say thank-you to all those people.'

So I put aside my initial angst and am now the proud possessor of the most beautiful and most expensive shirt I have ever bought or will ever buy, and I'm still asking myself, 'Was I right to buy it?'

What's so curious is that if I had a child who grew up to be a fashion designer I would be so proud; or if my child could cut a shirt just so; if my son knew how to grow the best-quality flax for the best-quality linen, or spent his days feeling swathes of cloth and separating the wheat from the chaff, as it were, I would be in tune with his passion. I'd also feel proud if he was an engineer on the Rolls-Royce design team, or an artist or sculptor. Yet there is a paradox: though as a society we love and indeed fall in love with 'creative' people, if we go out and *buy* what they make we are made to feel guilty. We become, by that act of putting our money where our mouth is, *consumers*, from the Latin word, *consumere* (not *consumare*), meaning not just to consume but more alarmingly *to devour, waste, squander, annihilate, destroy*. I can imagine a time when some socially responsible pressure group will argue that flax should no longer be grown 'to clothe the rich', when that land would be better used to 'feed the poor'.

But even if I am forgiven for spending £200 on a shirt, what if I had spent £200,000 on a new car? As before, I would be saying 'yes' to a whole host of people whose livelihood depends on that 'yes', and a further 'yes', indeed, to beauty, precision, excellence. I can't believe that I could persuade anyone that the buying of a hugely expensive car is moral; but is it actually immoral? And if it is, is it because so many people have nothing, or simply immoral *in itself*, regardless of one's personal wealth?

There used to be a virtue called *parsimony,* which was about making do with as little as you possibly could. My husband's family are all masters of parsimony: they even discovered a delicious gruel made of cattlefeed, which needs soaking for two days and slow-cooking for twelve hours before it becomes edible; but their food bill was scarcely more than £10 a week. In seventeen years of marriage, my husband's annual budget to spend on himself – books, CDs, sheet music, second-hand clothes on eBay, some with their previous owner's smell still lurking – is what I spend in one reckless moment. My fourteen-year-old son owns two pairs of jeans, two long-sleeved and two short-sleeved shirts, all from Tesco. He refuses anything more, and asks the price of clothes I want to buy him before allowing me to do so. For Christmas and birthday he asks for cash, which he saves. He even asked for cash instead of a Christmas stocking this year. Where did this son of mine come from? Should I feel proud or appalled?

A few years ago I was delighted to discover a possible answer to the shopping dilemma. In Dante's *Inferno* those who spend too little and those who spend too much inhabit the same circle of hell. I happily informed my husband that we were to be together for an eternity.

But with all my heart, I resist Dante's recommendation to be *moderate*. I don't want to be sensible all the time. Sometimes, when you see a beautiful painting and you just have to have it, isn't it *right* that you should throw caution to the winds?

food for thought

Q *Is extravagance only a vice in those who can't afford to be extravagant?*

Q *If your partner asks you how much you paid for something, would you always tell the truth?*

Q *Have you ever hidden something away for fear of being asked that very question?*

Q *Are you having an argument yet?*

Q *Do you think that spending a lot on good-quality food is more extravagant than spending it on something that will last a long time?*

Q *Do you prefer to spend money on 'objects' or 'experiences'?*

Q *Would you spend a lot of money on something just because it was beautiful? Or does it have to be useful?*

‘ on immortality ’

I wish pollsters didn't ask us such boring questions as, 'What party are you going to be voting for at the next general election?' Yawn, yawn. What they should really be asking us is, 'Would you like to be immortal?'

The answer would be fairly passionate one way or the other. Some would say that they couldn't think of anything more dreadful than to be shut into life and see their friends and children die one by one; while others would say, 'Surely that's what people have always craved – never to die?'

A couple of weeks ago I met a very rich businessman who was waxing lyrical about the possibility of living for ever. He had it all sorted – deep freezes, medical breakthroughs which might even reverse the process of ageing; he fancied an eternity at the age of about forty-two. My husband and I looked at him aghast. He accused us of having no spirit, no imagination. 'Think of all the amazing places there are still to see! How many amazing people there are to meet! Even, how many different kinds of food there are to taste!'

The difficulty for me would be how to be immortal meaningfully. Eternal pleasure would become a bit arduous after a century or two. It's bad enough having to make a pretty shape out of eighty years: though a good, time-worn one might be childhood, youth, marriage, work, children and grandchildren. Apart from 'work', the true business of life seems to be about love. To be open and intimate with others, at the best and worst of times, is all we can do to put meaning into our lives. Or perhaps, if one is truly noble, like a priest or philosopher-king or community worker, to help create the conditions in which openness and intimacy can thrive.

So what I would say to my businessman is that the only way he can carve out a meaningful niche for himself as an immortal is to become an angel.

food for thought

Q *Would you like to be immortal?*

Q *Would you like to be an angel?*

Q *What measures do you take to prevent your own death?*

Q *If it were destined that you should die on a particular day in a particular year, would you like to know now?*

Q *If you knew you were to die in six months' time, would you choose to live exactly as you are now, or have some great adventure?*

Q *If money was no object and there was a 10 per cent chance of being resurrected as a healthy human being, would you opt to be deep frozen after your death?*

Q *Do you believe in angels, or in some realm where 'spirits' exist outside time?*

' on mirrors '

What are we doing when we look at our own reflection? If you walk into a room and you catch a person looking intently into a mirror you are aware of interrupting something very private. I'm not talking about the business of shaving or applying lipstick; rather that of looking at yourself very, very hard and saying, 'This is who I am.' Or even, 'This is not who I am. This is how others see me.'

I've often wondered how people cope in houses with huge gilded mirrors hung on every wall: do they glimpse themselves happily every moment of the day? Are there people out there who would actually *choose* to sit in one of those urban cafes where they hang a vast mirror one foot in front of your nose? It's bad enough being confronted with yourself for a full hour in the hairdresser's. Yet no one complains.

It is an astonishing thing that a baby (or incidentally a chimp, dolphin, magpie or parrot) can look in the mirror and recognise itself. I remember as a small child sitting for hours, cross-legged and rapt, in front of the full-length mirror in my mother's bedroom. I surveyed every part of my body in minute detail, and the truth is, if you do that, you soon come to realise quite how weird and ugly the body of a human being is. Inside a nose, for example. Yuk! And ears that look like cauliflowers with holes in them, holes that lead right up into the brain. Yuk! And what's this stuff called skin? That also has little holes in it, and hairs, and the colour of 'white' flesh, between grey and pink, is probably the ugliest colour in the world. My hands, ridged, wrinkled, with hard bits on the end called 'nails' – yuk! My knees, wrinkled, scarred, yuk! Mouth, teeth . . . how strange they become when you look hard at them. A great, gaping hole, which leads right down into the stomach! What a disgusting, slimy thing the tongue is! And is this body actually *me* or is it *mine*?

Mirrors rub in the fact that there is an internal 'I' and an external shape, but what is the relationship between them? For me, I've always felt like a driver and what I see in the mirror is the car I'm driving; and the car was given to me, I didn't even choose it. Yet the world judges me by my car. What a terrible thought! That's why the mirrors in our house are very, very small.

I know myself as a subject; mirrors and the world know me as an object. Mirrors therefore turn out to be false friends (if ever they were your friends in the first place). Look briefly at them only for medical reasons. If there is too strong a connection between yourself and the person in the mirror, you will only know loss.

food for thought

Q *I often feel that I don't know what I look like, insofar as when I look in a mirror I regularise my face (remove*

smile/double chin, etc.) and look singularly unanimated. (How can I look 'pleased to see me'?) Do you feel you know what you look like?

Q *Do you quite enjoy looking in a mirror? Why, or why not?*

Q *If your partner came into the bathroom while you were having a critical look at yourself (hairs in nostril, blemishes on skin, etc.) would you feel embarrassed?*

Q *Do you feel that your face is you or yours?*

Q *Do mirrors make you feel too conscious of ageing?*

Q *Would you ever buy a large and very beautiful mirror for your home?*

Q *On a scale of 1 to 10, do you hate or like your reflection most of the time?*

❛ on democracy ❜

The right of every human being to live in a democracy was enshrined in the very first Universal Declaration of Human Rights in 1948: that's how sacred a cow it is. But unlike those other 'fundamental' human rights of the time – life, freedom, property, etc, it is not an end in itself; it is a means to an end. The true end of democracy is to elect a fair, strong and just government. There are two major obstacles to this: what if the people don't think that any political party is fair, strong and just? And secondly (which is what the hugely anti-democratic Plato argued), what if 'the people' put their own interests before, say, the interests of their country (to prevent their country's bankruptcy, for example) or the interests of the planet (let's make jam today, for tomorrow we die).

When I was a probation officer I made my young offenders sit round a large table and pretend they were Cabinet ministers. I would say, 'Crime has reached epidemic proportions. Come up with some suggestions to eradicate it once and for all.'

They were brutal. They were very keen, for example, to cut off the fingers of thieves, one for every time the thief got caught. There were to be no soft options *ever*. The Probation Service would be replaced by a top-notch armed police force, who would be given powers to kill a burglar on sight. They said we should bring back the stocks, and start humiliating offenders in public.

What if it were discovered that 60 per cent of the electorate agreed with them? Democracy is, literally, 'rule by the people' – in ancient Greece, the people literally did rule (well-born Athenian male citizens, anyway; even their 'President' was drawn by lot), but do we really want what the 'mob' wants? If we used our interactive televisions to vote for different policies on a Saturday night, with Simon Cowell introducing their various apologists and Cheryl Cole telling us in her charming Geordie lilt, 'You sound very dull this week, Kevin', or, 'We've seen that pensions routine before', or, more generously, 'This is certainly original! Our very first British-made guillotine! And who's the guillotine for, David, can you tell us that?'

So true democracy is something our government could do without, and probably we could all do without. The trouble is the government knows that too well and democracy has been reduced to a propaganda word with the same ring about it as 'Five Year Plan' might have had in the former Soviet Union – a project to keep everyone's spirits up but ultimately vacuous. There are simply too many people to satisfy. In Classical Athens the 'people' (male freeborn citizens) were physically present at the assembly, voting on this and that. But now it's not even possible to tell the political parties apart. It would be quite fun to take ten of Blair's policies, ten of Cameron's, put them all into a hat and ask schoolchildren to guess which policies were 'right wing' and which 'left wing'. I guarantee they would be no more clued up than I am, nor most of the electorate.

I've been able to vote for over thirty years yet always in a constituency with a safe majority. I've never felt I had one iota of power over any policy decision, however absurd. I once wrote a letter to the Transport secretary, Stephen Ladyman, telling him how I had driven at 34 m.p.h. in a 30 m.p.h. zone twice in two years, and if I were to be as reckless again and I lost my licence we would have to move house with five children and a dog because there's no public transport where we live. Was this just? I asked him. Might I opt for 120 hours' community service instead? He replied that if I drove more carefully in future those questions wouldn't have to be asked. O ye of little imagination!

So when people insist, 'We must all use the vote our forebears fought for!' I almost feel sad. Where there should be gratitude and pride, I find a great empty hole.

food for thought

Q *As a citizen in a democracy, do you feel you have any power to change things?*

Q *If being an MP was a career choice (with its own hurdles and exams and career structure) rather than one massive flirt with the electorate every five years, and the consequence was a stable, strong, if somewhat dull, government, would you have trouble with that?*

Q *My son has a 'suggestions box' in his school dining room, where he can tell the cooks what he likes and what he doesn't like, and suggest other menus. If you were*

to have a greater individual say in policy decisions, but abandoned the idea of a democratically elected government, would you, overall, feel you had greater or lesser power?

Q *If you knew for certain, rather than suspected, that most MPs are more concerned about how they're going to win the next election than running the country well, would you still support 'adversarial' politics, where policy is born of argument rather than consultation?*

Q *Would you make a good MP or Cabinet minister yourself? What would be your greatest concerns?*

❛ on lying ❜

When I was a girl, my grandmother said to me, 'Never lie, Olivia. Lying is a dreadful habit. Not because it's naughty, but because by lying to others you will end up lying to yourself.' This seemed as terrible a curse as having the wind change while you were pulling a face and being stuck with that face for ever.

For my grandmother, the decision to lie or not to lie was nothing to do with the behaviour society expected of you, but about self-knowledge. Visiting her was like visiting a holy shrine and I've instinctively lived by every observation she ever made. But the other day I was reading Dostoevsky's *The Brothers Karamazov* and there was my grandmother, in the form of the elder Zosima, who pronounces, 'Above all, don't lie to yourself. The man who lies to himself and listens to his own lie comes to such a pass that he cannot distinguish the truth within him, or around him, and so loses all respect for himself and for others. And having no respect he ceases to love, and in order to occupy and distract himself without love he gives way to passions and coarse pleasures, and sinks to bestiality in his vices, all from continual lying to other men and to himself.' Zosima's words seem to me wonderful, true and obvious; whether my grandmother had ever read them or had come to a knowledge of them at first hand, I shall never know.

Here is a test you can do by yourself:

Why do you think lying is wrong?

Is it (a) because you believe 'Do as you would be done by'? (Kant's Categorical Imperative)
Or (b) because you believe 'The sum total of happiness in a community is increased by there being trust'? (John Stuart Mill's *Utilitarianism*)
Or (c) would you rather go with Aristotle: 'I do not lie because I am not a liar'?

For myself, I don't lie because I'm not a liar. I like Aristotle's conception of virtue (he's the founder of what philosophers call 'virtue ethics') because you can go on being virtuous if you are the only person left in the world: you can go on being strong, brave and true.

I'm in the middle of an argument with a close friend of mine (which has so far lasted thirty years, and I should imagine will last thirty more) about whether I lie, or at least misrepresent the truth. She is an historian, I write fiction. When I tell a true story (is there such a thing?) I automatically rearrange the weight of the events so that the 'truth' of the episode emerges. My friend is suspicious of such a treatment of 'facts'. I say to her, 'I know you're right in a literal sense, but that doesn't mean I'm not telling the truth, and in fact eking out a more important truth than an historian might.' At which she rages, 'We will not know *the* truth until everyone in the world is dead. There might be a story one day, but not yet.' I plead with her that surely I'm allowed a lot of little stories, for now. 'But what are little stories,' she says, 'if not lies?'

food for thought

Q *Which to you would be a worse lie: if your partner were to ask you exactly what went on between you and X ten years ago after a party, and you said, 'Absolutely nothing' (when the truth was 'absolutely everything') because you realised the truth would jeopardise your marriage and you love your partner very much? Or: to claim for a camera you 'lost' on holiday from an insurance company when that camera had never even existed?*

Q *When and what was the last lie you told?*

Q *If your partner asked you, 'Do I look good in this?' and there was no way of returning the item to the shop, and the truth was, it made him / her look fat and sallow, what would you say?*

Q *Do you think that you are honest with yourself?*

Q *Do you think that what my grandmother and the elder Zosima say about 'lying to yourself' is true?*

Q *To whom would you look for 'truth' – the novelist or the historian?*

❛ on trust ❜

What is it that we are doing when we trust someone?

What is it that we are being when we are trustworthy?

To trust and be trustworthy are two sides of a terrifically complicated relationship. Indeed, there may not be a personal relationship at all, as in trusting an organisation to look after your money, and that organisation deserving that trust.

When I was a social worker 'trust' was a buzzword. Everyone must be taught how to 'trust' again. This irritated me hugely because while everyone was being taught how to trust, no one was being taught how to be trustworthy. In our very first 'induction day' as student social workers we all had to throw ourselves into each other's arms, and if we were not caught by the person who was, after all, a total stranger with whom we had had no prior relationship, we would break our backs. This still seems to me an absurd exercise; and at the time, I remember, I yearned to move away and break my partner's back just to prove a point. The exercise, as far as I was concerned, was more about *obedience to authority* (i.e. the staff running the course) than relationship.

So, what is it to 'trust' someone? It's about relinquishing alertness, letting down your guard and, ultimately, allowing another person to enter your very psyche. And we do it only after the most highly sophisticated, unconscious computation, the data of which are every experience you have ever had with every person you have ever met. In broken societies, trust doesn't even begin to exist, because what gives rise to it – the consistent and reliable behaviour of parents, friends and authority figures – doesn't exist.

There is also a content to trust, which makes things even more complicated. We trust in different ways each and every person we know: some we trust to post a letter; others to listen if we have a moral dilemma. When I worked with young offenders I trusted them not in the sense that I thought they were suddenly going to reform, but for something deeper than that. I felt that there was some place within them, no matter what crimes they had committed, which could be reached: a fundamental humanity, if you like. But I would never ask them questions: 'Did you do this? Did you do that?' because I could never trust them not to lie. Lying for most of them was a well-worn habit: it was what was beyond the lies that interested me. Call it a 'soul', if you like, which is why I wanted to be a probation officer in the first place: to seek out retrievable souls, the solid and real under the crap.

When I married my first husband, I took on board the possibility that he might leave me, but that didn't stop me trusting him, for the very same reasons I trusted offenders. We met too young, when we were eighteen and twenty-one, before he had had his fill of being adored by women. I thought he would grow up to be a great writer and would leave me for a young and beautiful fan when I was in my early forties. I would then live alone, have occasional lovers, and write popular philosophy books. But even though I suspected the marriage's eventual demise, I also knew that he was absolutely worth loving, trusting, and being hurt for.

food for thought

Q *Are you trustworthy? Would you remember to do some menial task for your partner? Is there a deeper way in which you should be trusted?*

Q *Has anyone in your life abused your trust? Has this damaged or strengthened you?*

Q *Have you been a trustworthy parent or friend? How guilty do you feel about having let somebody down?*

Q *Do you think it is more important to be trustworthy or to be able to trust?*

Q *Who do you trust most in the world? In what way do you trust them?*

Q *In what ways would you most like your partner to be trustworthy? Would you prefer him/her to be a good listener, or to remember to turn on the oven?*

' on therapy '

I confess I have a real problem with therapy. I have good friends who are therapists, and I've simply not dared to broach the subject with them because I know I would suddenly turn into someone I am not; I would fill to the brim with unspent rage. How unwise I was to begin writing this shortly before going to bed. I will not sleep.

This loathing and distrust of therapy began when I was training to be a therapist as part of my MA in Social Work. We were taught the methods of seven famous schools of therapy – Freud, Jung, Rogers, Transactional Analysis, Cognitive Therapy and a couple of others I can't remember – and told to choose the psychologist we felt most at home with, so to speak, before deciding what kind of therapist we would become. As all were writers with insight, I had no problem with reading their work, but to consider them as writers who were saying something *true*, to be swallowed whole and put into practice, seemed, in a word, bizarre.

The truth is I've always had a sceptical nature, which is why, in my book, philosophy trumps psychology. The bottom line is, 'How do we know anything at all?' Psychologists are fallible human beings: liable, therefore, to manipulate data to support a hypothesis. (Data where there is no agenda, when the research is purely descriptive, I have no problem with.)

When I was an undergraduate I once played a game amongst the psychology books of the University Library. The game went, find a thesis in one book, find its very opposite in another, and have them mutually destroy. The question I asked myself was, if I could have spent a couple of weeks sifting through the psychology corpus, how many books would be left by the end of it? And what would those books look like?

I have always held a core belief: that human beings flourish where there is intimacy, honesty, kindness, friendship. Psychologies that promote these values I trust – but you don't need a degree to know these things, they are there for everyone to see.

In fact, that's the very reason why I might be tempted to see a therapist: if there was a void in my heart when there should be warmth. If the therapist asked me to talk about my previous relationships, and revealed to me (or let me reveal to her, which is how good therapy works) that what was lacking in these relationships was intimacy, honesty, kindness, friendship, my 'transference' – i.e. my redirection of negative feelings towards my therapist which was formerly directed at parents, friends and partners, and which she would consider 'healthy' – would not actually be transference at all. It would be about the *new* relationship, that between me and the therapist. It will be the frustration I feel that I have been seeking a real intimacy all my life, which, though I divulge all my innermost secrets, I cannot even get from her, while she remains aloof, professional. Indeed, I'd feel utter rage and disappointment.

I suppose you shouldn't really go into social work as a sceptic. It's rather like entering the church as an agnostic.

But the crunch came when I had to do my practice placement. As a student probation officer, I had to apply the theory I had learnt in the classroom to a real caseload, and I had my own supervisor, Liz, to make sure I was doing so.

I had been asked to write a social enquiry report on a man of about twenty-two who had been caught by police riding his motorbike in an erratic manner ten months into a year-long disqualification. He was about to be sentenced, but the judge wanted to know whether there were mitigating circumstances.

The case was as straightforward as it could have been. I interviewed him. It transpired that the man had a partner, whom he loved very much. And then one day he'd come back from work to find a brand new washing machine in the kitchen. With no consultation whatsoever, she had spent the entire contents of their savings account on one item. He was furious with her. She was unrepentant. He slapped her. She ran outside into the dark. He felt awful, wretched at what he'd done, and wanted to find her and say sorry. He couldn't find her, and in his despair had gone out looking for her on his bike. End of story.

I wrote up my report, saying that I thought this was a one-off, and that in my view he hadn't been riding his bike prior to that. I recommended leniency.

But Liz didn't like my report at all. It was not theory-based. I had written it as a man in the street might have written it, and therefore it was 'unprofessional' and 'ignorant'. I asked her how she would have written it. She said, 'It's completely clear to me, as it ought to be to you. The man's bike is his penis. If he had found the girl, he would have raped her. You recommend leniency; I say the man is a rapist. The man is dangerous! And I have used theory to back up my argument. What theory have you been using, Olivia?'

I said I didn't need to use so-called 'theory'. I was a human being. And as a human being I could alternately imagine what it was like to be the woman wanting a new washing machine, and the man being angry with her for buying one without asking him. She shouldn't have bought it; he shouldn't have slapped her. It was an ordinary human story.

'You have learnt nothing!' she thundered. 'The government have wasted their money training you! And unless you write in your report that the man's motorbike is his penis, I am failing you!'

Well, I certainly wasn't going to stand up in court and explain why the man's motorbike was a penis, and I duly failed the placement.

The knowledge base of therapy seems so random to me – perhaps Liz turned out to be right, perhaps this man really *was* dangerous, but equally, one of the other 'therapies' on offer at my School of Social Work might have offered a different explanation for why this particular man rode his motorbike while disqualified. How can we ever find out the 'true' reason?

But my *real* problem with therapy is none of this. If it's in my nature to be sceptical about what knowledge of the human soul consists of, one thing I know for certain is that knowledge is power. And therapists imagine they have this 'knowledge', so can call themselves 'professional' and charge exorbitant fees: which means they have power over any unwitting client who comes along. The relationship becomes akin to a divine being and his subject, and love and dependence know no limit. And as is the way with divinity, He does not speak for hour upon hour, despite the protestations of His client, but when He finally pronounces His Word, bow down and obey! And why do intelligent people *submit*? Whatever happened to friends? What are the 'issues' that people have to 'work out' with a therapist, that a friend can't work out?

I have a friend who recently 'cracked up', for want of a better term. She is the absolute best; I confide in her absolutely, and I trust her absolutely. She now has a counsellor, a mental health nurse, and a psychiatrist.

This is her story. She was adopted as a baby. She had a very happy and stable childhood, but both her parents died when she was in her late teens. A man seemed to care for her, and she became his lover and had a child with him. But then the man began to drink, etc. and began to abuse her. She tried to escape from him but he always managed to find her. She was terrified, and even thought of killing him.

Along came a second man, who whisked her away in a white sports car. There were a dramatic few months of playing cat and mouse, but eventually they managed to shake the abuser off completely. They moved into a large house and her Rescuer even sent her child to a private school. For a few years, she was incredibly happy, incredibly in love.

Then one day, three years ago, they were staying in a five-star hotel in the Seychelles – a favourite haunt of theirs – and he told her he was leaving her and going to live in Czechoslovakia with another woman, who was expecting his baby. He disappeared into thin air, leaving no forwarding address.

Not only that but this Rescuer whom she so adored, and who seemed to have adored her, turned out to have been a swindler as well. All these years he'd been making her sign contracts which have left her with £800,000 worth of debt.

My friend's been in counselling for months. On the couch, she's still only five years old. She's told she must suffer from feelings of abandonment because she's adopted, and she tells the counsellor that she was never aware of feeling abandoned, only loved, but of course the counsellor knows best about these deeper psychic places so she shuts up. Last week was really bad. She relived her fifth birthday party, the day her much-beloved grandfather died. Her overwhelming sense of loss and pain at bringing up these old memories leaves her, she tells me, feeling suicidal. She couldn't even go into work for the rest of the week. But her counsellor insists it's 'all part of the healing process'.

Her counsellor would *know,* of course. And she knows about relational transactions, interpersonal motivational theory, ego states, constructivism, redecision and self reparenting.

Whereas I know nothing. Or rather, one word we all know: betrayal.

food for thought

Q *Have you ever been to a therapist or been tempted to go to one?*

Q *When counsellors from Europe, trained in 'trauma survival', fly out to visit countries after a tsunami / earthquake and offer victims their wisdom, do you have faith that they will really do some good?*

Q *Have you ever read a psychology book? Would you be interested in doing so?*

Q *Do a role play with your partner, taking it in turns to be the patient and the therapist. What kind of problem would you choose to discuss?*

Q *Is there anything that has happened to you in your life that you would be happy to discuss with a trained therapist but not with your partner?*

Q *Do you think I have been unreasonably harsh on the profession?*

‘ on love ’

Love is wonderfully complex. When I ask people, 'What is love?' they retort, 'What kind of love do you mean? The kind of love a parent has for a child? The being-in-love sort? The kind of love you find in a long-term relationship? Or the kind of love my partner has for his car?'

I say, 'All of those. I want a definition of love that can include every aspect of it.'

They tell me, 'Impossible. In fact, there ought to be different words for the different emotions, so different are the kinds of love.'

And, of course, people have used different words to express these different aspects of love: eros, affection, charity, friendship – all of these emotions we recognise, and they feel quite different. Yet still I can't resist trying to get to the very core of love – all these loves – to see if there is an essential ingredient, so to speak.

At the two poles, I would suggest, are 'Greek' love – an early version of 'romantic' love – and 'Christian' love, which is all about 'loving your neighbour as yourself'.

In Plato's *Symposium* one of his characters (Aristophanes)

talks brilliantly about what it means to experience *eros*. He tells the story of how Zeus, irritated that men weren't sufficiently submissive to his authority, decided to split the original model – four-armed, four-legged etc. – into two, thereby dooming man to spend his life looking for his other half so that he can become whole again:

> And so, when a person meets the half that is his very own, whatever his orientation, whether it's to young men or not, then something wonderful happens: the two are struck from their senses by love, by a sense of belonging to one another, and by desire, and they don't want to be separated from one another, not even for a moment.
>
> These are the people who finish out their lives together and still cannot say what it is they want from one another. No one would think it is the intimacy of sex – that mere sex is the reason each lover takes so great and deep a joy in being with the other. It's obvious that the soul of every lover longs for something else; his soul cannot say what it is, but like an oracle it has a sense of what it wants, and like an oracle it hides behind a riddle.

How wonderful is that? *Eros* is more than the physical desire for the body of another; it's a coming home for the soul itself. 'The soul of every lover longs for something else' – isn't this exactly what we mean by love?

But then compare this with the famous verses of St Paul read out at practically every wedding:

Love is patient, love is kind. It does not envy, it does not boast, it is not proud. It is not rude, it is not self-seeking, it is not easily angered, it keeps no record of wrongs. Love does not delight in evil but rejoices in the truth. It always protects, always trusts, always hopes, always perseveres.

Gosh. These might be terrific qualities in an MP or a community leader, but in a relationship are they sufficiently *personal*? Is it possible for someone to have all these qualities and still not really *love* his or her partner in the way we think of as 'love'? And why is it that in the personal ads in newspapers those supposedly seeking 'love' never mention 'protective, trustworthy, patient, calm' and prefer to meet someone 'slim' and with a 'good sense of humour'? And the truth is, I love my partner for his occasional rudeness, intolerance and pessimism. They make me feel like I'm living with a real human being, not some paragon that I can't relate to. The trouble with the Christian description of love is there isn't enough *movement* there, and when I think of love, and myself as the lover, be it of my partner, my children or my friends, above all I think of a certain 'oomph', a directional movement towards them.

Yet St Paul's are time-honoured verses, and we go back to them again and again. On the back of these Christian virtues – and love is the central thesis of Christianity – was built an entire civilisation which has lasted for two thousand years. They cannot be sneezed at.

So how can these two versions of the nature of love be reconciled?

The curious thing about the love described in the *Sym-*

posium is that the person yearned for seems to meet the exact, though mysterious specification of the person doing the yearning. In other words, the person yearned for is fulfilling a personal need. And in the myth, the lover is *relating* not to another human being at all, but to his 'other half', and the fit between them will be as snug as if they were one. Isn't this what happens in romantic love? Isn't the task in romantic love absolute possession – because the beloved *is* yours, whether they know it or not?

But romantic love is even bigger than that. If, at its inception, the lover merely projects all possible desirable qualities on to a blank and beautiful sheet, as it were, thus turning the beloved into an idol to be worshipped, the feeling invoked soon becomes akin to religious mania: the yearning, a yearning for God, no less. And in your imagination, once reunited with the missing part of your own soul, you will be one for eternity. No wonder there seems to be so much more of the directive 'oomph' I'm looking for than all the 'patience' and 'kindness' promoted in the Christian version of love.

Yet, I would argue, the goal (or *telos,* as in Greek) of both kinds of love is the same – namely *knowledge* of the beloved – and the 'oomph' I want for love is *the desire to know.* In the Bible, to 'know' a woman means to have sex with her, but in a deeper sense the drive to become acquainted with the intimate recesses of another's heart, and know it as well as you know your own, is love indeed.

In romantic love, this knowledge is akin to an instant recognition that 'this is the one'; hence all those muses for artists – beautiful creatures whose hearts must be possessed. But in Christian love the journey is very slow indeed, and may even take a lifetime. While romantic love is instantaneous and for ever, Christian love is rooted in time. If you look again at those ponderous virtues, patience, perseverance, protectiveness, they are actually about *letting something happen*. They are the opposite of controlling, of *making* something happen. And surely, parental love is very much akin to Christian love. It's about *getting to know your children*, slowly, truly, and over time.

The same is surely true about love between partners – it's the non-judgmental acknowledgement that there is *another person* in your life, not your missing other half, but someone else. And how do human beings get to know each other? If you're like me, I'm afraid, you ask questions – hence this book; but there is a far more brilliant way of getting to know someone, which is almost mystical. Human beings have the gift of imagination. We can *imagine* what it feels like to be someone else. We know what it's like to feel tired, and are therefore sympathetic to our partner's bad mood. We know what it feels like to be hopeful, and hope alongside our partner for whatever it is they're hoping for. When they've had a bad day at work and slump into a chair exhausted and fed up, we've already been there, we know what that feels like, so we get them a glass of wine and listen *patiently* to the travails of the day. To love someone is to *be right there with them*. To love someone, is the *desire to know* them.

This ability is our greatest human attribute. We can imagine what it might feel like to be our neighbour – hence we know what it means to love them as ourselves. We can even imagine what it feels like to be someone we've never met. And the Christian injunction to 'love your enemy' is as profound as it gets.

When I lived in Cambridge, I decided to try out this business of 'loving your enemy', and the enemy in question happened to be my neighbour. We lived in the centre of town, and parking was at a premium. In our street, which was a private lane owned by one of the colleges, we were the only house without a garage, and we used to park in front of three disused garages belonging to a neighbour who didn't own a car. Then one day a man moved in next door and asked this neighbour to lend him *all three garages*, and then told us, bad luck, we could no longer park where we'd been parking for the last ten years because he needed access to all three of 'his' garages at all times.

I tried the 'pity me' argument. I said, 'I have five small sons and when I go shopping at the supermarket, where do you suggest I park to unload?'

He said, 'That's not my problem', and when I decided to park there anyway he would wake me up in the dead of night and tell me to move my car.

So filled with hatred for this man, such as I have never felt for anyone, I could barely sleep at night. And then I understood exactly what it was I had to do.

How I managed to rise to the occasion, God alone knows, but as I walked to the man's front door that morning I felt no malice towards him whatsoever.

When he opened the door, he scowled.

I said to him, 'I need to tell you something extremely important.'

'Yes?' he said.

'I've come to say, I love you, and I want this all to be behind us.'

When I heard myself speak, what I said felt true. For

the first time I saw before me a *person*, a real live person that I had never noticed before.

'What do you propose?' he asked me.

'If you don't mind,' I said, 'I propose that we hug straight away.'

And we did hug. It was a hug for all time, lasting minutes. It was as heartfelt from him to me as it was from me to him. It was a hug between human beings, during which every iota of rage that we'd ever felt towards each other evaporated, as though it had only ever been as much hot air. And he told me the exact place where I might park my car. For ever and ever.

food for thought

Q *Do you think men and women love in different ways?*

Q *Among your friends, would you say there are some you 'like' and others you 'love'? What is the difference in the emotion?*

Q *Have you ever felt you loved a stranger?*

Q *Do you think I have a point, in seeing a connection between 'love' and 'knowledge'?*

Q *How highly do you esteem the experience of 'being in love'?*

Q *When you see older couples who are obviously still devoted to each other after years of marriage, do you have a sense that their love is more 'real' than the new, heady love of the young?*

‘ on step-families ’

One of the surprising things about being human is that the only way we can really learn about anything is by experiencing it. We cannot just read books. We cannot just listen to friends. We have to live through every painful experience first-hand to finally understand what is valuable in this life. I loved my first husband. He broke my heart: I watched it breaking. But what I underestimated entirely was how the demise of our marriage would affect our children. Our family was broken, too. A step-family is what happens when some cumbersome outsider tries to mend it with the wrong pieces.

The other day I read a line from Virgil's Aeneid, (Book 4, line 53) which made me sigh for what we as a society have lost. Dido has fallen in love with Aeneas, and is doing all she can to resist it. Her sister asks her this:

‘*Nec dulces natos Veneris nec praemia noris?*’

‘Will you never know sweet children or the prizes of Venus?’

The ‘sweet children’ are *of Venus* in the word order. Children are the ‘prizes’ of love. When did you last read that *anywhere*? If ever? Nowadays, we take precautions *against* children, and *then* we can enjoy Venus! In fact, sex and children have become so thoroughly divorced from one another that sometimes we seem to forget where children come from, and a return to the past seems less likely than the modern scenario of (safely) picking up your baby from the laboratory at term.

In fact, my first thought when meeting my second husband (we had been good friends at university, but had barely seen each other since) was not, 'Wow, you're so handsome, and I like you!' but 'Why aren't *you* the father of my children? Why did I get things so wrong?' And the feelings of loss which dogged me for years had little to do with missing my first husband and everything to do with that sense of completeness, which I only truly understood the moment it was gone.

So then, what do you do when you fall in love with someone who has children? The truth is, I had an easy time of it. We had lodgers. The lodgers came and went, and the children always loved them, and nagged them constantly to play – board games, football, *Uno*. I told the boys that if ever they wanted a lodger to stay forever I would marry them, and they had to choose the one. Twice they came as a little delegation to tell me they had reached a decision. They wanted me to marry a nice Scot called Graham or Grey-man as they called him. I said I'd think about it. Then two years after my first husband left, almost to the day, I had a new lodger called Mark. Mark took them to play football when he came back from work. Mark took them to buy the largest television any of us had ever seen. 'We've definitely decided now,' they told me.

I said to them, 'You know what, I think you might be right', and the three of them were my page boys.

But I wish a step-parent wasn't called a 'step-parent'. They are not parents, they are nothing like parents. They should have no votes in parenting matters at all. They should stick to their role of being amazingly wonderful, patient and generous lodgers, who play games with the kids.

If I were a child with a step-parent, every single nag which issued from their mouths would be a thorn in my flesh, but I don't think I would really understand why. It would be because something which had been whole and precious had been broken, and this interloper couldn't understand that, they just thought they could step into someone else's shoes. No amount of patient reasoning would do the trick. In fact, all reasoning would be anathema to me, because I'd know with my guts it was wrong.

Now I have a second family. My first family have left home, they're out there in the real world: flats, jobs, girlfriends, the works. What we have left seems immeasurably precious: we're a husband and wife, and we have two sons, the prizes of love.

food for thought

Q *Do you have direct experience of being part of a step-family? What advice would you give to a friend who was about to be a step-parent?*

Q *Do you think I'm being sentimental when I call children 'the prizes of love'?*

Q *Do you think that the nuclear family is a good way of organising society?*

Q *How hard would you try to keep a marriage together for the sake of the children?*

Q *Why are marriages so hard to fix when they're broken?*

Q *As a child, would you have preferred to live in a household where there were a lot of arguments but you had both parents, or in a single-parent family?*

‘ on feminism ’

I had never even heard of feminism until I went up to Cambridge, where of course I met ardent feminists who tried to convert me to their cause. Their arguments were rational, and made total sense, but I had been brought up in an era where women were women and men were men, and from my perspective, women had infinitely the better deal. The women of my childhood found children pretty irritating, on the whole; and though occasionally we were indulged we were far more often ignored. Who they loved was each other, and when they were together they would bitch and giggle and be bent double with laughing so much. They played golf together, tennis, did *The Times* crossword together in a matter of minutes, and were phenomenal Scrabble and bridge players. They baked each other cakes, grew their own vegetables – we were self-sufficient in vegetables and jam all year – and in the summer they would all go on holiday together, husbands and children in tow.

One word I never heard as a child was 'career'. The word they used was 'job', and the function of a 'job' was to provide money for the family. This is what their husbands did. And their husbands would get up at six in the morning for their 'commute' (for years if someone asked me what my dad did for a living I would say he was a 'commuter'), disappear into some nether region for twelve hours a day, and return home to be given a list of chores to complete before dinner at eight. The men in my extended family looked ill and grey, while their wives had a deep, healthy glow.

Both my grandfathers were dead before I was born, but their widows were not to be fooled with. My maternal grandmother, it was rumoured, knew the whole of *The Oxford Book of English Verse* off by heart, and from the age of about five I was made to learn a poem every week – Tennyson, Wordsworth and Edgar Allan Poe – and to her I owe my passionate and romantic nature. This was somewhat tempered by my paternal grandmother, who warned me that I was 'affected' and in danger of becoming a 'bluestocking', which would never do. In the 1920s, straight off the set of *Gosford Park*, this grandmother won an air race, a motor race and a point-to-point in one year. When I knew her best – in the 1960s and '70s – I was terrified of her. While in the south my family would happily shell homegrown peas together, my Lincolnshire grandmother would go out into the garden with her shotgun – she was a fine shot! – and shoot our supper: rabbits, pigeons, pheasants, guineafowl, which she would promptly skin, pluck and hang in the larder. She also kept hens. It was one thing to gather the eggs – I quite enjoyed that, going out with her in the early morning to see how many had been laid – and a basket of eggs and hay was quite charming. But occasionally she would swoop down and seize a hen, wringing its poor neck right in front of me, and when I gasped in horror, exclaim, 'You told me you liked roast chicken!'

I was certainly never expected to have a 'job' myself. Only divorced women and old maids – poor things – had one of *those*. My godmother was the manager of a local Mars factory, but as they lay together on their sunbeds, enjoying the dappled sunlight of a summer afternoon (while we children had gone off to make dens), my mother and her cousins would call her 'heroic' in pitying tones, while debating whether it was too early for a jug of Pimm's.

The main event of our annual TV calendar, more important even than the *Eurovision Song Contest*, was *Miss World*. My mother and I watched this from the comfort of her marital bed, while my father attempted to read some book about the Second World War while pushed right to the edge of the mattress. We even used little notepads to write down our comments, and took guessing the winner very seriously indeed. We were merciless. A bust was too big, a neck was too short, hips were invariably too wide. My mother always went for blondes, I preferred the dark-haired ones with Mediterranean complexions. We used to laugh when it was time for the interview. We took it for granted that if you were beautiful, you were probably going to be quite dim.

So when I met my first feminist, who railed against the 'cattle market' that was *Miss World*, I naturally kept quite quiet, and felt, I confess, a little shame; but when a couple of years later I met my first 'male chauvinist pig' as they were called, I laughed till I cried. I couldn't believe they really existed. By the end of the evening, I promise, every masculine bone in that poor man's body had been crushed, my Amazonian heritage suddenly springing to the fore.

So, the big question is, do men treat women as objects?

In the West, now as much as any time in history, if you're a woman your face is your fortune. Even the Communist French philosopher Alain Badiou begins his book *In Praise of Love* with an account of how there he was, minding his own business, when in walks a ravishingly beautiful woman and *pow!* he was in love, just like that. A woman doesn't need to say a word; the woman is beautiful: the woman is pure object.

Yet though I felt intense irritation reading Alain Badiou's account of how he tends to fall in love, isn't it also the case that women *present* themselves as objects? That they make a conscious decision about how much flesh to reveal, or how to adore their naked bodies? I can't believe that the recent fad for 'vajazzles' (if you don't know what they are, I can't bring myself to tell you) is to do with self-expression.

Moreover, if men objectify women, which they do, and women objectify themselves, which they do, is it not the case that women also objectify men? For some reason, women tend to go in for 'nice bums'. They also find wealth and power sexy. Isn't loving a man because he is powerful on the same moral trajectory as loving a woman for her perfect breasts?

When people complain that there aren't enough women in the higher echelons of the business world, and the implication is that they are being overlooked by the last remnants of a chauvinist culture, I always think it's because women don't *want* to be on every board going, they don't *want* to spend their lives in meetings when they might be lying in the garden instead with a couple of girlfriends and a glass of wine, musing on the meaning of life. In fact, it might just be that in fifty years' time, instead of the Hollywood diet we're fed nowadays of 1950s suicidal women bored with child-rearing and longing to go out to work, grisly scenes of exhausted mothers going out to work for twelve-hour days will appal us in much the same way.

food for thought

Q *Have either you or your partner ever counted yourself as a feminist? Why, or why not?*

Q *Do you think men tend to objectify women more than women objectify men, or do you think it's roughly equal?*

Q *Would the world be a better place if there were more women in government?*

Q *Do you think that men and women have different kinds of brain – in which case, how are they different? – or do you think our differences are entirely culture-based?*

Q *How much do you think Western women should help women from other cultures to attain equal status to men?*

❛ on the difference between laziness and relaxation ❜

If you were to come to my house at about two in the afternoon you would look through our glass front door and find an array of boots and coats all over the floor, various piles of letters and books, open drawers with gloves and scarves spilling out of them, and you would wonder if there'd been a burglary (indeed one such visitor reported that there had been).

Our door is generally open: if you're brave enough to come inside and walk upstairs you'll find me lying amongst five open books on my bed, glasses still on my nose, fast asleep. I would be having my daily siesta. So, how lazy am I?

The interesting thing about laziness is that *you*, as the observer, don't know how lazy I am. For all you know, I might have been up by six, taken the dog for a two-hour walk, and have written five half-decent pages. The only person who knows how lazy I am is myself, and this is the same for all of us. We all of us know when we are being lazy and when we are enjoying the fruits of industry: a good rest.

I have become an expert in distinguishing between these two conditions. When I relax, I love myself. When I am lazy, I hate myself. And it's quite impossible to deceive myself! It's that simple.

I know I have girlfriends who wonder, 'What *does* Olivia do all day?' Luckily my husband, if he's ever asked himself that question, has never asked me. (Otherwise he'd be done for.) But I'm very fair to myself. I know exactly what I deserve. And I was lazy yesterday. That's why I was up at five this morning – a Saturday – to rub wood stain into the pale, sad floor. Now I'm writing this, a glass of wine on the desk beside me. It's five to one. My bed and my books await.

Every individual is thermostatted differently, so to speak. How much relaxation are you allowed before guilt trips in? Luckily my mother, a great believer in the universal benefits of being 100 per cent relaxed, has given me a very high threshold. If I've done well for the first six hours of the day, both physically and mentally exerting myself, why, I don't even try to *read* in bed. I watch a Bette Davis movie, head snug against the pillows, rain pouring outside (suggesting that I shouldn't even weed the garden), happy as a sandboy. But if I haven't done well, if I've got down to nothing and even the dog is accusing me of neglect, self-indulgence sickens me, makes me feel fat and heavy and unhappy. I need to be punished, and in my catatonic state I devise ruthless punishments for myself, including major housework projects and violent gardening: no TV, no books, no pleasure of any sort, until I am thoroughly cleansed. It is at moments like these that even clearing up the dog's sick increases my spiritual well-being.

But why is it that the majority of my friends, even if they feel exhausted from the pressures of work and family, do not allow themselves to slip between the sheets till the last saucepan has been cleaned and put away?

I've never got to the bottom of this. I imagine it's some dreadful Protestant work ethic upbringing: do not rest until your house is immaculate! In other words, *do not rest.* Why do people put themselves through such a terrible torture? Cleaning a basin with three days' dirt on it takes a fraction of a second longer than if you were to clean it every day, and look at this blissful thing called time that is created as a consequence: time to do exactly as you please.

I've spent years trying to convince friends to let their standards slip, just a little. I've told them of the joys of feeling refreshed after a nap, as though the day has a new beginning. I've even mentioned the pleasures of cleaning the kitchen in the early hours of the morning when you can't sleep – and if the kitchen was already clean, what would there be to do but toss and turn? Knowing when to yield to moods and when to overcome them is a terrific art. I'm pleased I err on the side of yielding.

food for thought

Q *If I were your partner, would you get angry with me?*

Q *Why do you think people are so perfectionist when it comes to their houses?*

Q *On the day before my marriage, a reflexologist friend of mine gave me a foot massage, and told me that she'd never seen feet as relaxed as mine, not a single nodule of tension in either foot. I honestly think that counted as the proudest moment of my life. Was I ridiculous to have been so pleased with myself?*

Q *If you were feeling tense after a hard day's work, would you let your partner give you a massage?*

Q *If ever you feel that stodgy, lethargic laziness descend upon you like unwelcome humidity, how do you manage to shift it? Or do you simply succumb?*

❛ on death ❜

My mother thought that death was an excellent thing on two counts. Firstly, the fact that death existed at all made life more valuable, when otherwise it might become utterly tedious; and secondly, death had the power to release people from terrible suffering. Death was never taboo even for an afternoon in our family. We talked about people who had died (including my beloved grandmother) as though they were in the room; and though my mother grieved terribly for friends who died before her, she was never for a moment frightened to die herself. Her only fear, indeed, was that there should be life after death, in which case she was on a one-way ticket to hell.

When I was thirteen I decided to rehearse my own suicide; my theory being that, if I was brave enough to take my own life, what seemed merely life-by-accident (after all, I'd never asked to be born) would be life-by-decision. Every single day, for the rest of my life, would become something I had decided to embark on, rather than something that was merely happening to me. Suddenly life would be like an interesting film: I could walk out any time if things got really frightening – or I could hang in there to see if there was a happy ending.

I staged my 'suicide' at the Eton diving pool. A friend had invited me to swim there – her father was a housemaster – and as soon as I looked up at the array of diving boards I knew I had to seize my chance. The highest platform (higher by far than the springboard) gave me vertigo the first time I climbed the ladder, so I came down again to make the option of failing more difficult than the option of succeeding. I went round the swimming pool and said to everyone, 'Watch me! I'm going to dive off that top board there and do a record number of somersaults! Just you watch!' Then I climbed back up the ladder till I stood on the very top.

Well, there I was, arms outstretched like a swallow, feeling a heady power that I had never known before. I threw myself into the air, and God only knows what I actually *did* in the air, but such a belly-flop ensued that I spent a couple of days in bed just getting over it. But days nonetheless of total bliss, at last knowing for sure that I could die at will and therefore live at will. My life was finally mine.

Choosing to live, really live, makes you feel awake at last. You notice yourself switching on a light, and the whole experience becomes extraordinary. You watch the weather, not with your focus on a game of tennis or a barbecue, but with itself as the focus. Suddenly you just can't believe the sky: as you look upwards, deeply, deeply upwards, it is more beautiful than any work of art you have ever seen, and makes you understand how small and irrelevant you are. Nothing you do matters in the vast script of the universe, which is deliciously liberating; your life becomes a present to open and see what's inside, rather than a chain that keeps you in its grip.

But if such feelings are possible only in the knowledge that one day they will no longer be possible, and that death also has the power, at a single, magnificent stroke to redeem us from the depths of suffering, why are our feelings towards death more akin to fear than gratitude? Death is a holy thing, regardless of whether one is religious or not. It is a gateway to the other, even if the other is merely non-existence.

There seems to me a curious modern-day belief that I've never been able to get my head round: Man must fend off Death at all costs, because to live in intense suffering is better than not to live at all. I know that Christians have a particular relationship with suffering. I know it's part and parcel of the human condition, to the extent that some suffering, at least, makes us human, and none gives us no chance to grow. Yet even the religious have different views on how to treat those at the end of their lives. I went to a Christian Science school, and was taught that life was so precious that both the beginning of it and the end of it belonged to God, and that human interference in these matters was morally repugnant. In Greek tragedy there's a word for it. Men commit the sin of *hybris*, a supreme arrogance, when they make themselves equal to the gods. No good will come of it.

I find it really difficult when doctors argue that taking life – in other words, switching off life-support machines – is beyond their job description. 'Doctors save lives, they don't take them' is their argument.

Yet, imagine you have been fighting at the battle of the Somme, and your friend lies dying at your side. He has lost both arms and legs and is begging you to put him out of his misery. Do you say, 'Sorry, I'm your friend, and friends don't kill. You're on your own, mate.' Or is there something that kicks in, more than 'doctor', more than 'friend', something like 'human being'?

Our wisest philosopher on the subject of death was Epicurus, who lived two and a half thousand years ago. He's most famous for his doctrines on pleasure, arguing that 'pleasure is the first good and natural to us.' He was a great lover of life. But on the subject of death he writes:

1. When you are dead, you neither experience pleasure or pain.
2. The only thing bad for us is pain.

Therefore it is irrational to fear death.
Are you persuaded?

food for thought

Q *If it were possible to know the date of your own death, would you want to?*

Q *If you had a week to live, but were in good health, what would you choose to do with this time?*

Q *What have you learnt in this life that you would want to pass on to your friends or children before you die?*

Q *Do you feel you have quite a healthy attitude to death, or do you prefer not to think about it?*

Q *Have you ever experienced the feeling of wanting to throw yourself into oblivion, for example when you walk along the edge of a cliff?*

Q *Why do you think death remains taboo, in a way that sex no longer does?*

‘ on euthanasia ’

Last year my mother died. She'd fought for that death for two years: as she watched her faculties fade, she'd visited lawyers and doctors; all were powerless to help her as she slipped into dementia, incontinence, and almost total immobility from the neck down. She had a strong heart, and eventually she had to starve herself to death. We watched her. It was an unbearable sight. None of us were with her when she died. Her means of death cost £112,000 in privately-funded care home fees, while the NHS footed the bill as she recovered from unsuccessful suicide attempts.

Here is what I would like for my own death. When I am weary of this life, am old, infirm and unhappy, yet while my mind is still my own, I should like to invite a good woman to my home, perhaps a retired nurse or priest, who could talk to me about dying, in much the way a midwife might call on an expectant mother. Her first duty would be to coax me to live, but failing that she would help me to die.

If I were too weak to speak to my family myself, she would let them know of my intentions. In my last weeks of life – knowing that that's exactly what they were – I would be able to summon friends to say goodbye; I could talk to my children and grandchildren and wish them well after I leave them. I would make my peace, make known my regrets, relive my joys. Then on the appointed day, my family would all be there. There would be music. I should like to listen to 'Ich habe genug' – meaning, appropriately, 'I've had enough' – and other sublime music that would make us all cry. Poetry might be read, there might be prayers, and when the moment came I would be given a drink from a cup I might have chosen beforehand – I'm thinking now of my grandfather's small silver christening mug – and the taste would be like mead, whisky and honey. Only recently a retired nurse told me that in the 1940s they called the delicious concoction they gave to the terminally ill 'Miss Terminus'.

At that point, if my husband were still alive, I would send everyone else out of the room to be alone with him. He would then climb up on the bed to lie with me with no self-consciousness. He would be well and truly with me when I died.

Then after the funeral – with some of that vast sum that might have been spent on my 'care' – I would send the family and a few close friends on a retreat to the country, which I would have chosen beforehand with their help. There would be no electronic gadgetry. There would be books, and music and long walks, and they would take stock of their own lives as they remembered me.

It's so odd to think that my mother's version of death is the only one legally possible.

food for thought

Q *On average, an elderly person will need nine years of 'care' at the end of their life. Are you going to watch your faculties fade with grace and acceptance?*

Q *Is there a condition that you would find more intolerable than others – blindness, deafness, chronic pain, immobility, incontinence, dementia?*

Q *Why do you think our society insists that life* of whatever quality *is better than no life?*

Q *On the radio yesterday a researcher couldn't contain his delight on discovering that a man with 'locked-in syndrome' could imagine a game of tennis. (When electrodes were applied to his brain and he was asked to imagine it, a brain scan yielded markedly similar patterns to those of healthy subjects.) Should we rejoice with him that for those 87,600 hours of being 'locked in' his patient has at least been able to enjoy remembering a game of tennis he might have played in his heyday?*

Q *If you were an Angel of Mercy, would you let those vegetative patients who had no inner life die first, or would your mission be to relieve the suffering of those whose minds were intact?*

' on aspiration '

The world is made up of aspirers and non-aspirers. Aspirers like to do well in life. They succeed, and enjoy the fruits of their success: status, wealth, power. I am a non-aspirer, and I suppose the reason why most of my friends are non-aspirers like me is because they actually have the time to chat. They are the people with whom I have the best conversations; aspirers tend to be exhausted by working so hard. There is Mark, who has spent thirty years studying the nature of language, Katrina, a poet who lives amongst the fishermen of Northumberland, and Christopher, whose father was a priest and has spent his life test-driving the world's religions to see which comes closest to anything he might deem 'truth'. All have shunned wealth and power for a life that satisfies in other ways. We all agree that if we were Simon Cowell, who has, so the press tells us, one day off a year, we would slit our throats. We wouldn't know ourselves. We would be living a non-life.

These are my requirements for life worth living, in order of priority:

1. Absence of fear.
2. Good health.
3. Absence of hunger.
4. A room of my own.
5. A bed, table, chair, access to books, writing paper, pens and natural light.
6. Quiet.
7. Close and meaningful friendships.
8. A telephone.
9. A kettle and tea-bags.

I can't actually think of number 10. It did cross my mind to write 'private bathroom' but then I remembered all those intimate conversations in bed-and–breakfasts with people I might never have met while waiting to use the loo, and thought better of it. Apart from needing to boil my kettle, and to have a bedside light, I could do without electricity – and even the kettle and light I could do without, if needs must. Both my husband and I come from families who prefer cold houses: so do we, and only turn the heating on when it's three degrees or colder. We don't get broadband where we live, nor have mobile phone reception, so doing without modern technology would mean nothing to us. To live without fear, and to live with love: this is what ultimately matters. The actual monetary cost, therefore, of a good life is fairly minimal.

What's curious is that when I was a truant officer in 1985 for a year, the families I visited would have pretty much agreed with me. Perhaps they might have said 'TV' where I put 'books', but I recognised in them non-aspirers like me: what we all wanted was an easy life with not too many demands being made upon us. Climbing up that greasy pole only to slip down again: what was the point of that? In fact Buddhism says much the same thing, which is why so many disillusioned aspirers end up as Buddhists.

Before I made my first home visit I expected to find severely dysfunctional families and neglected children. I expected to befriend the children, send them back to school, and blame the parents. But time and time again I found myself agreeing with them. School was boring, they all told me, they couldn't see the point of it. If you were going to be a brain surgeon, fine, but otherwise, why sit at the back of a class that was going nowhere?

I listened, and I was persuaded. When the mother said, 'My son's a real help to me at home, he goes on errands, and helps me with the baby, all too often I would think, 'It's true, he's a sweet lad, perhaps he really is learning something here that he wouldn't at school.' Nonetheless, I persevered, employee of the state that I was. 'But what about getting some decent qualifications to set him up in life?'

'He's already got a job with his dad at the market,' I was told. 'He can add up anything in his head – you test him – and one day he'll take over the stall himself. And he can read, too. If you can read and write a bit and add up in your head, what else is education for? He wouldn't want one of those jobs like being a doctor. All that stress! What we want in life is to be happy, isn't it? Life's too short. And he's not happy at school. There's a lot of bullying that goes on at his school, and look how happy the lad is when he's at home.'

What can you say to a mum like her? How do you begin to argue your point? 'The government is embarrassed by the lack of social mobility, and needs your child to go to university, even if that means sacrificing his peace of mind and perhaps even his future happiness'? Because the truth is, back in 1985 the have-nots were surprisingly happy have-nots, and a good deal of baking and laughing went on. I want to suggest that non-aspirers might know something about life as lived that aspirers are completely ignorant of.

In fact, it even occurs to me that, if you take the 'aspiration' part of education out of education (i.e. the working hard, getting good results, going to a good university, getting a good job, earning good money, buying a nice house), you might just hit upon the ideal education, where a project title might be 'The full miraculousness of being human', and the purpose of such an education would be Conversation and Inquiry on every subject under the sun, with no tests, with no grades, and with no fear. There would be music galore, and dance, and the invention of recipes, and there would be a lot of talking and listening. The morale of teachers would rocket sky high, as children who arrived with nothing would visibly grow in confidence; and the older children would help to look after the younger children, in one vast support network. Funnily enough, this more or less describes my own education: free of aspiration, yes, but full of joy.

Speaking as a non-aspirer, I'd like to conclude this conversation with a heartfelt thank-you to all those aspirers out there who have made the gentle pace of my own life possible: first of all, both my husbands, and secondly, and no less importantly, all those aspirers who have worked hard and have paid their taxes. I would like to thank them personally for the NHS, free education for all, and for our magnificent armed forces. Don't listen to me when I describe the pleasure of leisure. Please, keep aspiring

food for thought

Q *All things being equal, would you say that you were by nature an aspirer or a non-aspirer?*

Q *What would your basic requirements be for a life worth living?*

Q *If you could afford not to work, would you give it up? If you did, how would you fill your days?*

Q *Have you ever yearned for the simple life?*

Q *If you were given a day to discover the recipe for a delicious soup, after spending a leisurely morning shopping at a market for fresh produce, would you have a good time?*

Q *Seeing that aspirers are so necessary for the rest of us, do you think it should be possible for potentially aspiring children to be given extra homework and private tuition (perhaps by non-aspiring volunteers like me, as a thank-you for our hope in them), and then, when they grow older, to be fast-tracked into thriving businesses?*

❛ on joining in ❜

Joining in is a very thorny issue for me. The truth is, I can't do it, not properly, not ever.

As a child, this is hell. There is a lot of joining in expected of a child. You have to join in the dancing. You have to join in the singing. For the record, between the ages of two and eighteen (my school career) I never joined in a single song, even with guitars round a camp fire, and I certainly never participated in the hymn-singing in the chapel where us girls were expected to sing at least once a day. I became an expert in mouthing words and acting the part of a girl who sang with gusto, only occasionally getting found out and humiliated.

My sister never joined in either, I discovered only yesterday when I asked her, and she has the added advantage of a beautiful voice that can carry a tune. She felt as bad about it as me. For our own offspring, we were both determined things would be different, and both of us (it turned out) had made spies of their nursery-school teachers, asking them to observe whether a single squeak emitted from our children's mouths. In seven case studies, nothing. The only conclusion is, we all suffer from a terrible genetic malfunction.

'Don't worry!' said my sister, 'Nobody joins in!'

'But a choir makes a noise, doesn't it? Why can't our family just let go?'

Yet if someone were to ask me the key to mental health, I would argue that it was to be part of something larger than oneself, to let down the barriers of being a solipsistic individual and join in with everyone else. No! Even as I typed those words, 'join in with everyone else', I knew I was lying. I don't want to join in with everyone else. I'm not going to. What am I frightened of? What am I resisting?

What I fear is being 'merely' part of a group, and losing some important sense of self. I know who I am. We get on perfectly well, I and myself, I know where I am with her, warts and all. If I let that sense of self go – and sometimes I can feel imprisoned by it, which is why a glass of wine is just the ticket – I might end up in a place which is worse, and lose control. I have never had any interest controlling others (I couldn't think of anything more tedious) nor tidying my house (perhaps that is actually more tedious), but my own mind is my own property, into which I invite others quite freely (as I'm doing now), and to leave it at the door of someone else's mind (or some 'group mind') is simply too much for me to bear.

Yet people really do enjoy being part of a team. I imagine that sense of 'we' is glorious. I watched the final stages of the *Tour de France* this year and was swept away by the team spirit: the individual sacrificing victory on behalf of all. Wow. When I used to play team sports at school my *only* concern was not to be shown up as being the worst player. Not an iota of me cared whether we won the game or lost it. It was my own personal battle.

Another cause for concern was fashion. Fashion was about joining in, wearing what everyone else 'in the know' was wearing. I rebelled furiously. I refused to even find out what you were supposed to be wearing, in case I should be 'sucked in' to wearing it. As a consequence, I remember wearing clothes my mother bought for me when I was seventeen and should have known better. I also rebelled by not smoking, when it was cool to smoke; refusing to enjoy sex, because everyone else was; cutting off the Green and Red thick cotton band from a Gucci handbag a suitor gave me in case anyone would brand *me* as the kind of person who would have a Gucci handbag; never going to a pop concert, because that's what other people did; never listening to pop music, because that *absolutely* sucked you in, like a drug. Basically, anything that had the power to take away my sense of being *me* I rejected. What fun I must have been!

What about the government's calls for us all to join the 'Big Society'? Great, really good. I'm not even a sceptic, I think it's a great thing. I once sat next to a man at dinner who had started a charity in Bury St Edmunds looking after young offenders the very second they were given a caution by the police – so kids of between ten and fourteen. They took them on outings, gave them outside interests, befriended them. In every way this seemed terrific: they had managed to prevent every single child, he told me proudly, from taking up a life of crime. (Five years later I met the man again and asked him how things were going. Badly, he said. The government had cut their £20,000 grant and it had proved impossible to raise money for 'young thugs'. The charity had closed down.) Yet if I were asked to give up just one evening a week, just one to help others less fortunate than me . . . I am exhausted just thinking about it. People are exhausting. Or rather, joining in is exhausting.

In Ancient Greece I would be punished for my attitude with exile or even death. Their near-perfect democracy had no room for people like me. In fact, the word for 'private citizen' is 'idiotes' in Greek, from which we get our word 'idiot'. I do my own thing. I don't have any interest in public office. I am irresponsible. I hide, and read and write in private. Even Aeschylus, the great playwright of the *Agamemnon*, preferred to remind posterity (in a simple epitaph on his tombstone) that he had fought at the battle of Marathon than bother us with the irrelevance of his *mind*, which was neither here nor there. In fact, it suddenly occurs to me that's why he wrote such terrific plays: he wrote them for the people to watch, enjoy, learn, feel; not as a means of 'self-expression', which would literally be 'idiotic'.

When I go to sleep at night and think of people I admire, they are rarely the clever-clogs of this world, rather those who give up their time for others out of kindness, whether voluntarily or because that's what life has flung at them. They are the *unsung heroes* of this life. And when I find myself crying at renditions of *Black Beauty* or *War Horse*, it's because the heroism of the dumb animal is *real*, it's a universal thing, and these stories can finally let us sing out and be amazed by unseen hands and unheard voices – all those people who do their bit for all of us, and whom we've never properly thanked or even recognised.

food for thought

Q *In what way are you good or bad at joining in?*

Q *If I were to tell you that tonight you'll be spending the evening*

    (a) at an exclusive night club in the King's Road
    (b) at a dinner party for ten with people you've never met before
    (c) at a supper with your partner and two close friends
    (d) in the kitchen with your partner
    (e) alone – in bed with a good book by half past nine

which would you choose?

Q *If you were asked to give up an evening a week to help in a soup kitchen, would you do so? How guilty would you feel if you said 'no'?*

Q *Do you feel it's your duty as a citizen in a democracy to vote at an election?*

Q *Do you wish you were less self-conscious?*

Q *Have you ever had the feeling of being part of a crowd? Did you enjoy it?*

‘ on cooking ’

Here are three particular conversations I have with my husband every few months:

(a) If we'd been adopted at birth by each other's parents, how would we have been different?
(b) If the world was populated by people only like you, darling, how would the world be different?
(c) What will you most miss about me after I'm dead?

When my husband first told me he'd miss me for my cooking I assumed he was joking. Then I hoped he was joking. Then I realised he was telling the truth. I said, 'That's like saying you'd miss me for my housework!'

'Oh no,' he said, 'it's not like that at all.'

My sister never learnt how to cook on principle. She imagined that from the moment she knew how, she'd be consigned to the kitchen forever. In fact, it turned out just as she hoped it would: her husband is an excellent cook, and they both love to eat out, and will describe a fine dinner to me, course by course. Meanwhile, the limit of my own husband's culinary expertise is to make himself peanut butter sandwiches. If I'm out for the evening, it's often too much for him (if the children aren't at home) to put a home-made (by me) shepherd's pie in the oven. Is he in my power, or am I in his? Probably both, this is just how we do things.

I remember our interview in the Register Office when we married in 1993. The Registrar asked me for my occupation. I had just finished my first novel and had submitted it as a manuscript for the Betty Trask Prize. 'What do you think, Mark? Am I a writer or a housewife?'

We both paused. I was unpublished. I made hardly any money writing: at most, a thousand pounds a year. I told the Registrar, 'Write "housewife" and Mark didn't object. When we came back from honeymoon, I found I had both a prize and a publisher, but it was too late, I was already a housewife.

Yet over these twenty years I have learned that Mark is right and my sister is wrong. Cooking can absolutely be lifted from the debris of mere maintenance. If a housewife is wedded to her house, a cook is wedded to everyone who enters it.

Oddly enough, for someone who loves to cook, I wouldn't count myself as a 'foodie'. I don't 'source' my meat and fish: and I buy from butchers and fishmongers more out of affection for the old-fashioned high street than because these things 'taste better' than Tesco's Finest. There are also several foods that I simply dread: all shellfish (because my mother used to make me listen to them squeaking in pain as they were being boiled alive); rabbits, hares, pigeons, doves, game, duck (because my grandmother on my father's side used to kill all these with her shotgun and hang them in her larder) and finally those foods the ancient Romans used to rave about: dormouse, flamingo and quail, which luckily one doesn't see too often nowadays. So you can see quite what a pathetic gourmet I am.

Yet cooking is the greatest pleasure I know of. I love my saucepans, all enormous and heavy, some dating from my first wedding list in 1982. When I chose them my girl-friends laughed. 'There are only two of you,' they said. 'Just you wait. I'm going to have six hefty sons, perhaps even seven because I like the name Septimus. I shall *need* pans this size.'

I love my wooden chopping boards, one French, one Swiss, both dating from about 1950. I love my knives, heavy and beautifully balanced. I love cutting vegetables, I love the feeling of the blade against a swede or a turnip. I love cutting meat. My mother taught me that the meat closest to the bone was the most succulent, so I buy shoulder of lamb and shin of beef, and spend many happy hours mus-ing on life while I remove the fat. I love growing fresh herbs and going out into the garden at twilight with my scissors. I love the sixty jars of herbs and spices which I keep in a single small cupboard. In fact, the only way I keep sane in a supermarket is to seek out the 'World Foods' section and buy a packet of something I have never heard of. Yesterday I bought a pack of ajwain seeds for thirty-two pence and put them in my carrot salad. Quite delicious.

In the end I stuck at five sons, but the eldest bring back their girlfriends and often we're ten at every meal. Even stirring the pot with a large wooden spoon makes me hap-py. I don't think it's possible to feel more absolutely human in any one moment: I use my nose, my eyes, my fingers, my tongue (for how can you cook without tasting every few moments?) and my imagination. Cooking is like writing or painting, but greater than either: it involves both the mind and every sense you were born with. And above all, cooking is about the heart, and the reason you're cooking in the first place: to feed those you love. So, Mark, it turns out you were right. If you miss my cooking when I'm dead, you're missing me.

food for thought

Q *I love to experiment: mixing one ingredient with another just to see what happens. And of course, experiments fail. Do you enjoy the element of risk in cooking, or avoid it?*

Q *I am always conscious of how much a meal costs. Last week I cooked a bag of green lentils on Monday and we had:*

> *Lentil and spinach omelette on Monday*
>
> *Lentil and potato curry on Tuesday*
>
> *Lentils in fresh tomato sauce with chilli and saucisson sec on Wednesday*
>
> *Lentils with mushrooms and wild rice on Thursday*
>
> *Lentil, cumin and lamb stew on the Friday*

All this came to under forty pounds and I felt very pleased with myself. Do you take pleasure in being an economical cook, or is it a greater priority to have top-notch quality, and organic food if possible?

Q *I love to read cookery books but rarely follow a recipe – that requires too much shopping and discipline. What is your relationship to cookery books?*

Q *My mother loved to cook too: I never 'learned' how to cook as such, merely imitated, and all five of my sons have followed suit. The saddest thing about fast food, it seems to me, is that the skills and joy of cooking are being lost. Does the ability to cook seem a precious one to you, or redundant in the modern world when there is so little time and so many good quality ready-made meals available?*